‘far too
noisy,
my dear
Mozart’

A collection of historical insults

Compiled by Jennifer Higgie

'far too noisy, my dear Mozart'

Special Edition for PAST TIMES®, Oxford, England

First published in Great Britain in 1997 by
Michael O'Mara Books Limited
9 Lion Yard
Tremadoc Road
London SW4 7NQ

A CIP catalogue record for this book is available from
the British Library

ISBN 1-85479-247-4

1 3 5 7 9 10 8 6 4 2

Designed by Mick Keates
Typeset by Concise Artisans
Printed and bound in England by Clays Ltd, St Ives plc

‘contents’

By God no, if it had been, I should have run away myself.

The Duke of Wellington (1769-1852) replying to a question from the Russian ambassador on whether Beethoven's Battle Symphony was like the actual battle of Waterloo

Wagner was a monster. He was anti-Semitic on Mondays and vegetarian on Tuesdays. On Wednesday he was in favour of annexing Newfoundland, Thursday he wanted to sink Venice and Friday he wanted to blow up the Pope.

❛on music❜

Tony Palmer on Richard Wagner (1813-83)

I like Wagner's music better than any other music. It is so loud that one can talk the whole time without people hearing what one says. That is a great advantage.

Oscar Wilde (1854-1900) on Richard Wagner

Wagner, thank the fates, is no hypocrite. He says out what he means, and he usually means something nasty.

James Gibbons Huneker on Richard Wagner

Wagner's music is better than it sounds.

Mark Twain (1835-1910) on Richard Wagner´

Is Wagner actually a man? Is he not rather a disease? Everything he touches falls ill: he has made music sick.

Friedrich Wilhelm Nietzsche (1844-1900) on Richard Wagner

Of all the bête, clumsy, blundering, boggling, baboon-blooded stuff that I ever saw on a human stage, that last night beat – as far as the story and acting went – all the affected, sapless, soulless, beginningless, endless, topless, bottomless, topsiturviest, tuneless, scrabble-pipiest-tongs and boniest-doggerel of sounds I ever endured the deadliness of, that eternity of nothing was deadliest, as far as its sound went.

John Ruskin (1819-1900) on Richard Wagner

Wagner has beautiful moments but awful quarter hours.

Gioacchino Rossini (1792-1868) on Richard Wagner

I love Wagner, but the music I prefer is that of a cat hung up by its tail outside a window and trying to stick to the panes of glass with its claws.

Charles Baudelaire (1821-67) on Richard Wagner

Composition indeed! Decomposition is the proper word for such hateful fungi.

Dramatic and Musical World (1855) on Franz Liszt (1811-86)

He writes the ugliest music extant.

Dramatic and Musical Review (1843) on Franz Liszt

Liszt's bombast is bad; it is very bad; in fact there is only one thing worse in his music, and that is his affected and false simplicity. It was said of George Sand that she had a habit of speaking and writing concerning chastity in such terms that the very word became impure; so it is with the simplicity of Liszt.

Philip Hale, Boston music critic, on Franz Liszt

He was fiddler and consequently a rogue.

Jonathan Swift (1667-1745)

Perhaps it was because Nero played the fiddle, they burned Rome.

Oliver Herford (1863-1935)

Berlioz composes by splashing his pen over the manuscript and leaving the issue to chance.

Frédéric Chopin (1810-49), Polish composer, on Hector Berlioz (1803-69), French composer

Berlioz, musically speaking, is a lunatic; a classical composer only in Paris, the great city of quacks. His music is simply and undisguisedly nonsense.

Dramatic and Musical Review (1843)

I can compare *Le Carnival Romain* by Berlioz to nothing but the caperings and gibberings of a big baboon, over-excited by a dose of alcoholic stimulus.

George Templeton Strong, British critic, diary entry

Jazz: Music invented for the torture of imbeciles.

Henry van Dyke (1852-1933)

It's bad when they don't perform your operas – but when they do, it's far worse.

Camille Saint-Saëns (1835-1921) on Dame Ethel Smyth (1858-1944), composer

Of all the bulls that live, this hath the greatest ass's ears.

Elizabeth I (1533-1603) on John Bull (c.1563-1628), musician

Far too noisy, my dear Mozart, far too many notes...

Archduke Ferdinand of Austria on Wolfgang Amadeus Mozart (1756-91)

After Rossini dies, who will there be to promote his music?

Richard Wagner on Gioacchino Rossini

[on music]

The audience seemed rather disappointed: they expected the ocean, something big, something colossal, but they were served instead with some agitated water in a saucer.

Louis Schneider on *La Mer* by Claude Debussy (1862-1918)

I liked the bit about quarter to eleven.

Erik Satie (1866-1925), composer, on 'From Dawn to Noon on the Sea' from *La Mer* by Claude Debussy

It is gaudy musical harlotry, savage and incoherent bellowings.

Boston Gazette on Franz Liszt

A glorified bandmaster.

Sir Thomas Beecham (1879-1961), British conductor, on Arturo Toscanini (1867-1957), Italian conductor

She would be like Richard Wagner if only she looked a bit more feminine.

Osbert Sitwell (1892-1969), poet and writer, on Dame Ethel Smyth

A tub of pork and beer.

Hector Berlioz, French composer, on George Friedrich Handel (1685-1759), German-born British composer

The musical equivalent of blancmange.

Bernard Levin, British journalist, on Frederick Delius (1862-1934), British composer

A provincial Debussy.

A. J. P. Taylor, British historian, on Frederick Delius

Splitting the convulsively inflated larynx of
the Muse, Berg utters tortured mistuned
cackling, a
pandemonium
of chopped-up
orchestral sounds,
mishandled
men's throats,
bestial
outcries,
bellowing,
rattling, and all
other evil
noises... Berg is
the poisoner of the
well of German music.

Germania on Alban Berg (1885-1935), Austrian composer

Beethoven always sounds like the upsetting
of bags – with here and there a dropped
hammer.

John Ruskin (1819-1900) on Ludwig van Beethoven (1770-1827)

Oh you arch-ass – you double-barrelled ass!

Ludwig van Beethoven on Gottfried Weber, music critic

I liked your opera. I think I will set it to music.

Ludwig van Beethoven to a fellow composer

Shostakovich is without doubt the foremost composer of pornographic music in the history of art.

W. J. Henderson, music critic, on Dmitri Shostakovich (1906-75)

... it is impossible to deny that his music (?) is a soporific, by the side of which the telephone book is a strong cup of coffee.

Samuel Chotzinoff on Alban Berg (1885-1935)

He was ignored till he began to smash the parlour furniture, throw bombs and hitch together ten pianolas, all playing different tunes, whereupon everyone began to talk about him.

Henry T. Fink, American music critic, on Arnold Schoenberg (1874-1951)

A composer for one right hand.

Richard Wagner on Frédéric Chopin (1810-49)

He sang like a hinge.

Ethel Merman on Cole Porter (1892-1964)

Listening to the Fifth Symphony of Ralph Vaughan Williams is like staring at a cow for forty-five minutes.

Aaron Copland on Ralph Vaughan Williams (1872-1958)

Rachmaninov's immortalising totality was his scowl. He was a six and a half foot scowl.

Igor Stravinsky (1882-1971), Russian composer, on Sergei Rachmaninov (1873-1943), Russian composer

The musical equivalent of St Pancras station.

Sir Thomas Beecham (1879-1961), on Edward Elgar (1857-1934), British composer

His wantonness is not vicious. It is that of a great baby, rather tirelessly addicted to dressing himself up as Handel or Beethoven and making a prolonged and intolerable noise.

George Bernard Shaw (1856-1950), on Johannes Brahms (1833-97)

What a giftless bastard!

Peter Tchaikovsky (1840-93) on Johannes Brahms

❪on music❫

Art is long and life is short; here is evidently the explanation of a Brahms symphony.

Edward Lorne on Johannes Brahms

Anton Bruckner wrote the same symphony nine times (ten actually), trying to get it right. He failed.

Edward Abbey on Anton Bruckner (1824-96), composer

If he'd been making shell cases during the war it might have been better for music.

Camille Saint-Saëns on Maurice Ravel (1875-1937)

If Beethoven's Seventh Symphony is not by some means abridged, it will soon fall into disuse.

Philip Hale, Boston music critic, in 1837 on Ludwig van Beethoven (1770-1827)

The singers and crew are not only useless in themselves, but spread about at large their contagious effeminacy.

William Cobbett (1763-1835), journalist, agricultural reformer, soldier and radical politician, on Italian singers in London

What is art? Prostitution.

Charles Baudelaire (1821-67)

Who is this chap? He drinks, he's dirty, and I know there are women in the background.

Lord Montgomery (1887-1976), on Augustus John (1878-1961)

Le Dejeuner sur l'herbe – this is a young man's practical joke, a shameful sore not worth exhibiting in this way.

Louis Etienne, French critic, on the painting by Edouard Manet (1832-83)

❛on art❜

To the service of the most wildly eccentric thoughts, he brings the acerbity of a bigot... his mental temperament is that of the first Spanish Grand Inquisitor. He is a Torquemada of aesthetics... he would burn alive the critic who disagrees with him.

Max Nordau (1849-1923) on John Ruskin

⸢on art⸥

I have seen and heard much of Cockney impudence before now; but never expected to hear a coxcomb ask two hundred guineas for flinging a pot of paint in the public's face.

John Ruskin (1819-1900) on James McNeill Whistler (1834-1903), American painter

... a life passed among pictures makes not a painter – else the policeman in the National Gallery might assert himself. As well allege that he who lives in a library must needs die a poet. Let not Mr Ruskin flatter himself that more education makes the difference between himself and the policeman when both stand gazing in the Gallery.

James McNeil Whistler (1834-1903), painter, on John Ruskin (1819-1900), critic

If people dug up remains of this civilisation a thousand years hence, and found Epstein's statues and that man [Havelock] Ellis, they would think we were just savages.

Doris Lessing (b.1919), South African writer, on Jacob Epstein (1880-1959), British sculptor

He bores me. He ought to have stuck to his flying machines.

Auguste Renoir (1841-1919) on Leonardo da Vinci (1452-1519)

There is one thing on earth more terrible than English music and that is English painting.

Heinrich Heine (1797-1856), German poet and essayist

He will never be anything but a dauber.

Titian (c.1490-1576) on Tintoretto (1518-94)

Epstein is a great sculptor. I wish he would wash, but I believe Michelangelo *never* did, so I suppose it is part of the tradition.

Ezra Pound (1885-1972), American poet

I mock thee not, though I by thee am mocked;
Thou call'st me madman, but I call thee blockhead.

William Blake (1757-1827) on John Flaxman (1755-1826), sculptor

Rembrandt is not to be compared in the painting of character with our extraordinarily gifted English artist, Mr Rippingille.

John Hunt, 19th-century art critic, on Rembrandt (1606-69)

The properties of his figures are sometimes such as might be corrected by a common sign painter.

William Hogarth (1697-1764), British painter, satirist and engraver, on Antonio Correggio, 16th-century Italian painter

A monstrous orchid.

Oscar Wilde (1854-1900) on
Aubrey Beardsley (1872-98)

He is nothing but a peeping Tom, behind the coulisses and among the dressing rooms of ballet dancers, noting only travesties on fallen womanhood, most disgusting and offensive.

The Churchman on Edgar Degas (1834-1917),
French painter

Shockingly mad, madder than ever, quite mad.

Horace Walpole (1717-97), British letter writer and memoirist, on Henry Fuseli (1741-1825), Swiss-born British artist

Just explain to Monsieur Renoir that the torso of a woman is not a mass of decomposing flesh, its green and violet spots indicating the state of complete putrefaction of a corpse.

Albert Wolff, critic, on Auguste Renoir (1841-1919)

Mr Lewis' pictures appeared to have been painted by a mailed fist in a cotton glove.

Dame Edith Sitwell (1887-1964) on Wyndham Lewis (1884-1957)

This is not amusing, it is dismaying and disheartening. The other day, someone attributed to me the statement that 'the human race was nearing insanity'. I never said that but if anyone is trying to convince me that this is 'modern art', and that it is representative of our time, I would be obliged to think that statement is true.

Kenyon Cox, American critic, in *Harper's Weekly* (1913) on Henri Matisse's painting 'The Red Studio'

It makes me look as if I were straining a stool.

Winston Churchill (1874-1965) on a portrait of him by
Graham Sutherland (1903-80)

His pictures seem to resemble not pictures
but a sample book of patterns of linoleum.

Cyril Asquith, British critic, on Paul Klee (1879-1940)

Daubaway Weirdsley.

Punch (February 1895) on Aubrey Beardsley (1872-98), British
artist and author

As for M. Cézanne, his name will be forever
linked with the most memorable artistic
joke of the last fifteen years.

Camille Mauclair, critic, on Paul Cézanne

A decorator tainted with insanity.

Kenyon Cox, American critic, in *Harper's Weekly* (1913) on Paul Gauguin (1848-1903), French painter

If this is art it must be ostracised as the poets were banished from Plato's republic.

Robert Ross, British critic, in the *Morning Post* (1910) on Vincent van Gogh (1853-90)

Of course we all know that Morris was a wonderful all-round man, but the act of walking round him has always tired me.

Max Beerbohm (1872-1956) on William Morris (1834-96)

My dear Whistler, you leave your pictures in such a sketchy, unfinished state. Why don't you ever finish them?

Frederic Leighton (1830-96), British painter, on James McNeil Whistler (1834-1903)

My dear Leighton, why do you ever begin yours?

James McNeil Whistler on Frederic Leighton

Rossetti is not a painter. Rossetti is a ladies maid.

James McNeill Whistler, American painter, on Dante Gabriel Rossetti (1828-82), British poet and painter

Mr Whistler has always spelt art with a capital 'I'.

Oscar Wilde (1854-1900) on James McNeil Whistler

I have been to it and am pleased to find it more odious than I ever dared hope.

Samuel Butler (1835-1902) on a Dante Gabriel Rossetti exhibition

It resembles a tortoiseshell cat having a fit in a plate of tomatoes.

Mark Twain (1835-1910) on J. M. W. Turner's 'The Slave Ship'

George the First was always reckoned
Vile, but viler George the Second;
And what mortal ever heard
Any good from George the Third?
When from Earth the Fourth descended
(God be praised!) the Georges ended.

Walter Savage Landor (1775-1864) on the Four Georges of England

'on royalty and aristocracy'

He has the heart of
a cucumber fried
in snow.

Ninon de Lenclos, French
courtesan, on the Marquis de
Sévigné, French aristocrat

... a pig, an ass,
a dunghill, the
spawn of an
adder, a basilisk,
a lying buffoon,
a mad fool with
a frothy mouth.

Martin Luther (1483-1546) on
Henry VIII (1491-1547)

🄵on royalty and aristocracy🄵

George the Third,
Ought never to have occurred.
One can only wonder
At so grotesque a blunder.

Edmund Clerihew Bentley (1875-1956) on George III (1738-1820)

The church's wet nurse, Goody Anne.

Horace Walpole (1717-97), British letter writer and memoirist,
on Queen Anne (1665-1714)

Here lies our mutton-loving king,
Whose word no man relies on;
Who never said a foolish thing,
And never did a wise one.

John Wilmot, Earl of Rochester, on King Charles II (1630-85)

Queen Victoria was a like
a great paper-weight that
for half a century sat
upon men's minds,
and when she was
removed their ideas
began to blow all
over the place
haphazardly.

H. G. Wells (1866-1946)
on Queen Victoria
(1819-1901)

A corpulent voluptuary.

Rudyard Kipling (1865-1936) on Edward VII (1841-1910)

Henry VIII perhaps approached as nearly to the ideal standard of perfect wickedness as the infirmities of human nature will allow.

Sir James Mackintosh, historian, on Henry VIII (1491-1547)

A more profligate parson I never met.

George IV (1762-1830) on Revd Sydney Smith (1771-1845)

I am unwell. Bring me a glass of brandy.

George, Prince of Wales (1762-1830), in 1795 on having kissed for the first time his bride-to-be, Princess Caroline of Brunswick (1768-1821)

No danger. For no man in England would take away my life to make you king.

Charles II (1630-85) to his brother the Duke of York (1633-1701) on being warned by him of the danger of walking about unprotected

Now at least I know where he is.

Queen Alexandra (1844-1925) to Lord Esher shortly after her husband Edward VII (1841-1910) had died

My dear firstborn is the greatest ass, and the greatest liar and the greatest canaille and the greatest beast in the whole world and I most heartily wish he were out of it.

Queen Caroline (1683-1737) on her son Frederick, Prince of Wales (1707-51)

Yes. I do think the bloom of her ugliness is going off.

Colonel Disbrowe, chamberlain to Queen Charlotte, wife of George III, on the slight improvement in her looks as she grew older

She was happy as the dey was long.

Chief Justice Lord Norbury on Queen Caroline's affair with the Muslim Dey of Algiers in 1820

He would fain be a Despot, even at the cost of another's Underling... I look on him as one of the moral Monsters of History.

Samuel Taylor Coleridge (1772-1834), British poet, on Charles II (1630-85)

Throughout the greater part of his life, George III was a kind of consecrated obstruction.

Walter Bagehot (1826-77), English historian, on George III (1738-1820)

The wisest fool in Christendom.

Henri IV (1553-1610), first Bourbon King of France, on James I (1566-1625) of England

A dull, stupid and profligate King, full of drink and low conversation, without dignity of appearance or manner, without sympathy of any kind with the English people and English ways and without the slightest knowledge of the English language.

Justin McCarthy, Irish journalist and writer, on George I (1660-1727)

Here lies Fred,
Who was alive and now is dead:
Had it been his father,
I had much rather;
Had it been his brother,
Better than another;
Had it been his sister,
No one would have missed her;
Had it been the whole generation,
Better for the nation:
But since 'tis only Fred,
Who was alive and is dead –
There's no more to be said.

Horace Walpole (1717-97), English writer, on Frederick, Prince of Wales (1707-51)

Cursed Jezebel of England.

John Knox (1505-72) on Mary I (1516-58)

Very sorry can't come. Lie follows by post.

Telegram from Charles Beresford to the Prince of Wales (1894-1972), later Edward VIII, following a dinner invitation at short notice

Alvanley – who's your fat friend?

George Beau Brummel (1778-1840), British dandy, of George IV (1762-1830)

Born into the ranks of the working class, the new King's most likely fate would have been that of a street-corner loafer.

James Keir Hardie (1856-1915), British Labour politician, on George V (1865-1936)

The plain truth is, that he was a most intolerable ruffian, a disgrace to human nature, and a blot of blood and grease upon the History of England.

Charles Dickens (1812-70) on Henry VIII (1491-1547)

You have sent me a Flanders mare.

Henry VIII on seeing Anne of Cleves (1515-57) for the first time

Queen Anne was one of the smallest people ever set in a great place.

Walter Bagehot (1826-77), British constitutional historian, on Queen Anne (1665-1714)

I cannot find it in me to fear a man who took ten years a-learning of his alphabet.

Elizabeth I (1533-1603) on Philip II of Spain (1527-98)

Nowadays a parlour maid as ignorant as Queen Victoria was when she came to the throne would be classed as mentally defective.

George Bernard Shaw (1856-1950) on Queen Victoria (1819-1901)

What is there in the delivering over of a purgid blockhead and an unprincipled prostitute into the hands of the hangman that it should arrest for a moment attention.

Robert Burns (1759-96) on the execution of Louis XVI (1754-93) and Marie Antoinette (1755-93)

King William blew his nose twice and wiped the royal perspiration from a face which is probably the largest uncivilised spot in England.

Oliver Wendell Holmes (1809-94), American writer, on William IV (1765-1837)

❝on royalty and aristocracy❞

A noble, nasty course he ran,
Superbly filthy and fastidious;
He was the world's 'first gentleman',
and made the appellation hideous.

Winthrop Mackworth Praed on George IV (1762-1830)

Most gracious Queen, we
thee implore
To go away and sin no
more,
But if that effort be too
great,
To go away at any rate.

Anon. epigram on Caroline of
Brunswick (1768-1821), wife of George IV

A more contemptible,
cowardly, selfish
unfeeling dog does
not exist than this king... with vices and
weaknesses of the lowest and most
contemptible order.

Charles Greville, English diarist, on George IV (1762-1830)

His intellect is of no more use than a pistol
packed in the bottom of a trunk in the
robber infested Apennines.

Prince Albert (1819-61), Consort of Queen Victoria, on Edward,
Prince of Wales (1841-1910)

Who is this Pope I hear so much about? I cannot discover what is his merit. Why will my subjects not write in prose?

George II (1683-1760), on Alexander Pope (1688-1744), British poet

Strip your Louis Quatorze of his king gear, and there is left nothing but a poor forked radish with a head fantastically carved.

Thomas Carlyle, Scottish historian and essayist, on Louis XIV (1638-1715)

In private life he would have been called an honest blockhead.

Lady Mary Wortley Montagu (1689-1762) on George I (1660-1727)

The most notorious whore in all the world.

Peter Wentworth, English MP, on Mary, Queen of Scots (1542-87)

Henry IV's feet and armpits enjoyed an international reputation.

Aldous Huxley (1894-1963) on King Henry IV (1366-1413)

For seventeen years he did nothing at all but kill animals and stick in stamps.

Harold Nicolson, English diplomat and writer, while writing his biography of George V (1865-1936)

𝒇on royalty and aristocracy 𝟃

As just and merciful as Nero and as good a Christian as Mohammed.

John Wesley (1703-91) on Elizabeth I (1533-1603)

Damn the North! and damn the South! and damn Wellington! The question is, how am I going to get rid of this damned Princess of Wales.

Prince of Wales (1762-1830), later George IV, on a political marriage for him despite his private marriage to Mrs Fitzherbert

Trust a Brahman before a snake, and a snake before a harlot, and a harlot before an Afghan.

Traditional Hindu saying

An Englishman will burn his bed to catch a flea.

Traditional Turkish proverb

❛on proverbs and curses❜

Cursed be your mother's anus. Cursed be your father's testicles.

Traditional Yoruba verbal duelling curse

I shit on the balls of your dead ones.

Traditional Spanish gypsy curse

A waste of skin.

Traditional Lancashire expression

on proverbs and curses

Shake a bridle over a Yorkshireman's grave and he will rise and steal a horse.

Traditional Lancashire saying

He lied like an eye witness.

Russian proverb

After shaking hands with a Greek, count your fingers.

Traditional Albanian saying

There are only two types of Chinese – those who give bribes and those who take them.

Russian proverb

England: a good land and a bad people.

Traditional French saying

As sluttish and slatternly as an Irishwoman bred in France.

Traditional Irish saying

Half an Italian is one too many in a house.

Traditional French and German insult

Italy is a paradise inhabited by devils.

Traditional German saying

An ass in Germany is a professor in Rome.

Traditional German saying

Make one sign of the cross before an
Andalusian and three on sighting a Genoese.

Traditional Spanish saying

A Lithuanian is not worth a cheap slipper.

Traditional German saying

Did hogs feed here or did Lithuanians have
a feast here?

Traditional Polish saying

The Lithuanian is stupid like a pig but
cunning like a serpent.

Traditional Polish saying

❲on proverbs and curses❳

The devil seduced Eve in Italian. Eve misled Adam in Bohemian. The Lord scolded them both in German. Then the angel drove them from Paradise in Hungarian.

Traditional Polish saying

A single Russian hair outweighs half a Pole.

Traditional Russian saying

The Pole is there to oppress and the peasant to endure.

Traditional Ukrainian saying

The Pole is a thief; the Prussian a traitor; the Bohemian a heretic; and the Swabian a chatterbox.

Traditional Ukrainian saying

The Russian knows the way, yet he asks for directions.

Traditional German saying.

Be friendly with the Russian, but take care that you have a rock ready on your chest.

Traditional Ukrainian saying

May you wander over the face of the earth forever, never sleep twice in the same bed, never drink water twice from the same well, and never cross the same river twice in a year.

Traditional gypsy curse

The Spaniard is a bad servant, but a worse master.

Traditional English saying

The only good that comes from the east is the sun.

Traditional Portuguese saying

He who would eat in Spain must bring his kitchen along.

Traditional German saying.

Die, may he: Tiger, catch him; Snake bite him; Steep hill, fall down on him; River, flow over him; Wild boar, bite him.

Traditional curse of the Todas of South India

God made serpents
and rabbits and
Armenians.

Turkish saying

May your left ear wither
and fall into your right
pocket.

Traditional Arab curse

May you melt off the
earth like snow off
the ditch.

Traditional Irish curse

May you dig up your father
by moonlight and make soup of his bones.

Traditional Fiji Islands curse

May the curse of Mary Malone and her nine
blind illegitimate children chase you so far
over the hills of Damnation that the Lord
himself can't find you with a telescope.

Traditional Irish curse

May you be cursed with chronic anxiety
about the weather.

John Burroughs (1837-1921)

The indigested vomit of the sea
Fell to the Dutch by just propriety.

Andrew Marvell (1621-78), English poet, in *The Character of Holland* (c.1664)

America is one long expectoration.

Oscar Wilde (1854-1900)

'on people and places'

What a pity it is that we have no amusements in England but vice and religion.

Revd Sydney Smith (1771-1845)

❝on people and places❞

The way to endure Summer in England is to have it framed and glazed in a comfortable room.

Horace Walpole (1717-97)

There are in England sixty different religions and only one sauce.

Carraciolo (d.1641)

I have been trying all my life to like Scotchmen and am obligated to desist from the experiment in despair.

Charles Lamb (1775-1834)

Much may be made of a Scotchman, if he be caught young.

Samuel Johnson (1709-1784)

Their demeanour is invariably morose, sullen, clownish, and repulsive. I should think there is not, on the face of the earth, a people so entirely destitute of humour, vivacity or the capacity for enjoyment.

Charles Dickens (1812-70) on Americans

I never saw an American man walk or stand well; they are nearly all hollow chested and round shouldered.

Frances Trollope (1780-1863), British writer

Of course, America had often been discovered before Columbus, but it had always been hushed up.

Oscar Wilde (1854-1900)

If I owned Texas and Hell, I would rent out Texas and live in Hell.

General Philip H. Sheridan (1831-88)

This gloomy region, where the year is divided into one day and one night, lies entirely outside the stream of history.

W. W. Reade on Canada in 1872

❝on people and places❞

The purity of the air of Newfoundland is without doubt due to the fact that the people of the outports never open their windows.

J. G. Millais on Newfoundland in 1907

A rascally heap of sand, rock, swamp, called Prince Edward Island, in the horrible gulf of St Lawrence; that lump of worthlessness... bears nothing but potatoes.

William Cobbett (1763-1835)

So this is Winnipeg. I can tell it's not Paris.

Bob Edwards (1864-1922) on Winnipeg

Niagara Falls is simply a vast, unnecessary amount of water going the wrong way and then falling over unnecessary rocks.

Oscar Wilde (1854-1900)

I suppose there is less alms-giving in America than in any other Christian country on the face of the globe. It is not in the temper of the people either to give or to receive.

Frances Trollope (1780-1863)

The American has no language. He has dialect, slang, provincialism, accent and so forth.

Rudyard Kipling (1865-1936)

In Russia a man is called reactionary if he objects to having his property stolen and his wife and children murdered.

Winston Churchill (1874-1965)

You know that these two nations are at war for a few acres of snow, and that they are spending... more than all Canada is worth.

Voltaire (1694-1778)

The Americans,
like the English,
probably make
love worse than
any other race.

Walt Whitman (1819-92)

Kick all
America in
the guts: they
need it...
Spit on
every
neurotic... All that arty and literary crew,
I know them, they are smoking, steaming
shits.

D. H. Lawrence (1885-1930) in a letter to Mabel Dodge Luhan
on America

England, the heart of a rabbit in the body of
a lion.
The jaws of a serpent, in an abode of
popinjays.

Eugene Deschamps (14th century) on England

The perfidious, haughty, savage, disdainful,
stupid, slothful, inhospitable, inhuman
English.

Julius Caesar Scaliger (1540-1609) on England

❛on people and places❜

You must look out in England that you are
not cheated by the charioteers.

Marcus Tullius Cicero (106-43 BC)

It is related of an Englishman that he
hanged himself to avoid the daily task of
dressing and undressing.

Johann Wolfgang von Goethe (1749-1832) on the English

What I got by going to Canada was a cold.

Henry David Thoreau (1817-6?)

Our nation is divided into two species: the
one of idle monkeys who mock at
everything; and the other of tigers who tear.

Voltaire (1694-1778) on France

˹on people and places˺

It is by the goodness of God that in our country we have those three unspeakably precious things: freedom of speech, freedom of conscience and the prudence never to practise either of them.

Mark Twain (1835-1910)

In unimportant trifles, he deals in the most puerile and endless distinctions, while in matters of utility not to say matters of science, it [the Javanese language] is utterly defective... It wantons in exuberance, when species, varieties and individuals are described – while no skill is displayed in combining and generalising.

John Crawford, orientalist and colonial administrator, on the Javanese language (1820)

America... where laws and customs alike are based on the dreams of spinsters.

Bertrand Russell (1872-1970)

The Javans' income is frittered away by being wasted on the vile herd of miscreants and vagabonds belonging to the Hindu village under the various and incongruous appellations of astronomers, doctors, poets, musicians, barbers and dancing girls.

John Crawford comparing the Javanese peasant to the Hindu peasant (1820)

They are 'lazy and listless... they rise about half past seven or eight o'clock in the morning. They spend the fore-noon in toying and playing with their female slaves while a few moments afterward they will have the poor creatures whipt most unmercifully for the merest trifle. They loll in a loose and airy dress upon the sofa.'

John Crawford on the offspring of oriental female slaves and Europeans in the Dutch East Indies (1820)

We know no spectacle so ridiculous as the British public in one of its periodical fits of morality.

Thomas Babington Macaulay (1800-59)

England and America are two countries divided by a common language.

attr. George Bernard Shaw (1856-1950)

on people and places

One thing I will say for the Germans, they are always perfectly willing to give somebody else's land to somebody else.

Will Rogers (1879-1935)

English Fair Play is a fine expression. It justifies the bashing of the puny draper's assistant by the big hairy blacksmith, and this to the perfect satisfaction of both parties, if they are worthy of the name of Englishman.

Joseph Furphy, Australian novelist (1903)

The English are the people of consummate cant.

Friedrich Wilhelm Nietzsche (1844-1900)

The English never smash in a face. They merely refrain from asking it to dinner.

Margaret Hasley, American writer

I spent a horrid, horrid night. I dreamt I was chained to a rock and being talked to death by Harriet Martineau and Macaulay.

Revd Sydney Smith (1771-1845) on Thomas Babington Macaulay (1800-59), British historian, and Harriet Martineau (1802-76), British philanthropist and writer

The great apostle of the Philistines.

Matthew Arnold (1822-88) on Thomas Babington Macaulay

on historians

You know, when I am gone, you will be sorry you never heard me speak.

Sydney Smith to the notoriously garrulous Thomas Babington Macaulay, British historian

JONNARD.

🖡on historians🖢

He not only overfilled with learning but stood in the slop

Thomas Carlyle (1795-1881) on Thomas Babington Macaulay

The same old sausage, fizzing and sputtering in its own grease.

Henry James (1843-1916) on Thomas Carlyle

Another thick square book! Always scribble, scribble, scribble! Eh! Mr Gibbon!

William, Duke of Gloucester to Edward Gibbon (1737-94)

Gibbon is an ugly, affected, disgusting fellow and poisons our literary club for me. I class him among infidel wasps and venomous insects.

James Boswell on Edward Gibbon

Gibbon's style is detestable; but it is not the worst thing about him.

Samuel Taylor Coleridge (1772-1834), British poet, on Edward Gibbon

They told me how Mr Gladstone read Homer for fun, which I thought served him right.

Winston Churchill (1874-1965) on William Ewart Gladstone (1809-98)

It was said Mr Gladstone could convince most people of most things, and himself of anything.

Dean William R. Inge on Gladstone

❝on politicians❞

... was brilliant to the top of his army boots.

David Lloyd George (1863-1945) on Douglas Haig (1861-1928), British field marshal

Oh, if I could piss the way he speaks!

Georges Clemenceau (1841-1929) on David Lloyd George

on politicians

If he were a horse, nobody would buy him; with that eye, no one could answer for his temper.

Walter Bagehot (1826-77), British constitutional historian on Lord Henry Peter Brougham (1778-1868), British statesman and author

One could drive a schooner through any part of his argument and never scrape against a fact.

David Houston, American politician, on William Jennings Bryan (1860-1925), American lawyer and politician

A lamentably successful cross between a fox and a hog.

James G. Blaine, American politician, on Benjamin Franklin Butler (1818-93), American soldier

Dr Dread-Devil ... said that there were no trees in Scotland. I wonder how they managed to take him around without letting him see trees. I suppose that that lick-spittle Boswell, or Mrs Piozzi, tied a bandage over his eyes when he went over the country which I have been over. I shall sweep away at this bundle of lies.

William Cobbett (1763-1835) on Samuel Johnson (1709-84)

A Winston Churchill who had never been to Harrow.

H. G. Wells (1866-1946) on Huey Pierce Long, American politician

God damn your god damned old hellfired
god damn soul to hell god damn you and
god damn your god damned family's god
damned hellfired god damned soul to hell
and good damnation god damn them and
god damn your god damned friends to hell.

Peter Muggins, American citizen, letter to President Abraham
Lincoln (1809-65)

Filthy Story-Teller, Despot, Liar, Thief,
Braggart, Buffoon, Usurper, Monster,
Ignoramus Abe, Old Scoundrel, Perjurer,
Robber, Swindler, Tyrant, Field-Butcher,
Land-Pirate.

Harper's Weekly on Abraham Lincoln

You and I were long
friends; you are now my
enemy and I am
Yours,
Benjamin Franklin

Benjamin Franklin (1706-1790)
to William Strahan

With death doomed to
grapple
Beneath this cold slab, he
Who lied in the Chapel
Now lies in the Abbey.

Lord Byron (1788-1824) on William Pitt (1759-1806)

That dark designing sordid ambitious vain
proud arrogant and vindictive knave.

General Charles Lee (1731-83) on George Washington (1732-99)

... a hypocrite in public life,
the world will be puzzled to
decide whether you are an
apostate or an impostor,
whether you have
abandoned good
principles, or whether
you ever had any?

Thomas Paine (1737-1809) to
George Washington

He was essentially a prig, and among prigs there is a freemasonry which never fails. All the prigs spoke of him as the coming man.

Benjamin Disraeli (1804-81) on William Ewart Gladstone (1809-98)

He has committed every crime that does not require courage.

Benjamin Disraeli on Daniel O'Connell (1775-1847), Irish lawyer, politician and agitator

Douglas can never be president, Sir. No, Sir; Douglas never can be president, Sir. His legs are too short, Sir. His coat, like a cow's tail, hangs too near the ground, Sir.

Thomas Hart Benton (1782-1858) on Stephen A. Douglas, presidential candidate

Wallowing in corruption like a rhinoceros in an African pool.

E. L. Godkin (1831-1902) on James G. Blaine, American politician

He was oppressed by metaphor, dislocated by parentheses and debilitated by amplification.

Samuel Parr (1747-1825) on a speech by Edmund Burke (1729-97)

... he insults the House of Lords and plagues the most eminent of his colleagues with the crabbed malice of a maundering witch.

Benjamin Disraeli (1804-81) on the Earl of Aberdeen (1784-1860)

❮on politicians❯

They inculcate the morals of a whore and the manners of a dancing master.

Samuel Johnson (1709-84) on Lord Chesterfield's letters of advice to his son

He is like a carving knife whetted on a brickbat.

John Randolph (1773-1833) American politician, on Ben Harden, American politician

His face is ashen, gaunt his whole body,
His breath is green with gall;
His tongue drips poison.

Ovid (43 BC-AD 17), applied by John Quincy Adams (1767-1848) to John Randolph

Every drop of blood in that man's veins has eyes that look downward.

Ralph Waldo Emerson (1803-82), American philosopher and poet, on Daniel Webster, American politician

We did not conceive it possible that even Mr Lincoln would produce a paper so slipshod, so loose-joined, so puerile, not alone in literary construction, but in its ideas, its sentiments, its grasp. He has outdone himself.

Chicago Times (1863) on Abraham Lincoln's Gettysburg Address (19 November 1863)

A crafty and lecherous old hypocrite whose very statue seems to gloat on the wenches as they walk the States House yard.

William Cobbett (1763-1835), on Benjamin Franklin (1706-90), American statesman and scientist

He has all the characteristics of a dog except loyalty.

Sam Houston, American politician, on Thomas Jefferson Green (1801-63), American politician

He has a bungalow mind.

Woodrow Wilson (1856-1924), 28th American president on Warren Harding (1865-1923), 29th American president

The General is suffering from mental saddle sores.

Harold L. Ickes, American Secretary of the Interior, on Hugh S. Johnson (1882-1942), American soldier

The style of all pestilential filth that hath infested the state and government of this commonwealth.

Sir Harbottle Grimston, British MP, on William Laud (1573-1645), English clergyman and Archbishop of Canterbury

Gladstone appears to me one of the contemptibilist men I ever looked on. A poor Ritualist; almost spectral kind of phantasm of a man.

Thomas Carlyle (1795-1881), Scottish historian and essayist on William Ewart Gladstone (1809-98)

What is that fat man in such a passion about?

Lord Eversley as a child in the gallery of the House of Commons, in G.W.E. Russell, *Collections and Recollections* (1898) on Charles James Fox (1749-1806), British statesman

You show the bourgeoisie your behind. We, on the contrary, look them in the face.

Georgi Plekhanov, Russian Social Democrat, on Vladimir Ilyich Lenin (1870-1924), Soviet leader

Like rotten mackerel by moonlight, he shines and stinks.

John Randolph, American politician, on Edward Livingstone (1764-1836), American politician

He is a self-made man and worships his creator.

attr. John Bright on Benjamin Disraeli (1804-81)

If a traveller were informed that such a man was the leader of the House of Commons, he might begin to comprehend how the Egyptians worshipped an insect.

Benjamin Disraeli (1804-81), British prime minister and author, on Lord John Russell (1792-1878), British prime minister

His impact on history would be no more than the whiff of scent on a lady's handkerchief.

David Lloyd George (1863-1945) on Arthur Balfour (1848-1930)

My one ardent desire is that after the war he should be publicly castrated in front of Nurse Cavell's statue.

Lytton Strachey (1880-1932) on David Lloyd George

I thought him fearfully ill-educated and quite tenth rate – pathetic. I felt quite maternal to him.

Hugh Walpole (1884-1941) on meeting Adolf Hitler (1889-1945) in 1925

... and to you, sir, treacherous in private friendship ... and a hypocrite in public life, the world will be puzzled to decide whether you are an apostate or an impostor, whether you have abandoned good principles or whether you ever had any.

Thomas Paine (1737-1809), letter to George Washington (1732-99)

His smile is like the silver fittings on a coffin.

Benjamin Disraeli (1804-81) on Robert Peel (1788-1850)

He only had one idea and that was wrong.

Benjamin Disraeli on a now forgotten MP

He is a mere cork, dancing in a current which he cannot control.

Arthur Balfour (1848-1930), British prime minister on Henry Campbell-Bannerman (1836-1908), Liberal prime minister

Not a gentleman. Dresses too well.

Bertrand Russell (1872-1970) on Anthony Eden (1895-1977)

He spent his whole life in plastering together the true and the false and therefrom manufacturing the plausible.

Stanley Baldwin (1867-1947) on David Lloyd George (1863-1945)

Sir Stafford has a brilliant mind until it is made up.

Lady Violet Bonham-Carter (1887-1969) on Sir Stafford Cripps (1889-1952)

I met murder on the way –
he had a mask like Castlereagh.

Percy Bysshe Shelley (1792-1822) on Viscount Castlereagh (1769-1822), British foreign minister (1812-22)

Mr Gladstone speaks to me as if I were a public meeting.

Queen Victoria (1819-1901) on William Ewart Gladstone (1809-98)

I thought he was a young man of promise;
but it appears he was a young man of promises.

Arthur James Balfour (1848-1930) on Winston Churchill (1874-1965)

Like a cushion he always bore the impress of the last man who had sat on him.

David Lloyd George on Lord Derby (1865-1948) (also attr. to Lord Haig)

This goat-footed bard, this half-human visitor to our age from the hag-ridden magic and enchanted woods of Celtic antiquity.

John Maynard Keynes (1883-1946) on David Lloyd George (1863-1945)

The right honourable and learned gentleman has twice crossed the floor of this House, each time leaving behind a trail of slime.

David Lloyd George on Sir John Simon (1873-1954)

I think Baldwin has gone mad. He simply takes one jump in the dark; looks around and then takes another.

Lord Birkenhead (1872-1930) on Stanley Baldwin (1867-1947)

A tardy little marionette.

Randolph Churchill (1849-95) on Clement Attlee (1883-1967)

If Kitchener was not a great man, he was at least, a great poster.

Margot Asquith (1864-1945) on Lord Kitchener (1850-1916)

One could not even dignify him with the name of a stuffed shirt. He was simply a hole on the air.

George Orwell (1903-50) on Stanley Baldwin (1867-1947)

Stupid asses.

Karl Marx (1818-83) to Friedrich Engels (1820-95),
private correspondence, on the proletariat

on politicians

That grand impostor, that loathsome hypocrite, that detestable traitor, that prodigy of nature, that opprobrium of mankind, that landscape of iniquity, that sink of sin, that compendium of baseness who now calls himself our Protector.

Anabaptists' address to Charles II on Oliver Cromwell (1599-1658)

Posterity will ne'er survey
A nobler grave than this;
Here lie the bones of Castlereagh:
Stop, traveller, and piss.

Lord Byron (1788-1824) on Viscount Castlereagh, British foreign minister (1812-22)

... as thin as the homeopathic soup that was made by boiling the shadow of a pigeon that had been starved to death.

Abraham Lincoln (1809-65) on the ability of Stephen A. Douglas (American politician) to reason

He is a silk stocking filled with dung.

Napoleon Bonaparte (1769-1821) on Charles Maurice de Talleyrand-Périgord (1754-1838), French statesman and diplomat

How can they tell?

Dorothy Parker (1893-1967) on hearing that American President
Calvin Coolidge (1872-1933) had died

He lived a hypocrite and died a traitor.

John Foster, English historian, on Oliver Cromwell (1599-1658),
Lord Protector of England

A cold-blooded, calculating, unprincipled usurper, without a virtue; no statesman, knowing nothing of commerce, political economy, or civil government, and supplying ignorance by bold presumption.

Thomas Jefferson (1743-1826), American president, on
Napoleon Bonaparte

If Gladstone fell into the Thames, that would be a misfortune, and if anybody pulled him out that, I suppose, would be a calamity.

Benjamin Disraeli (1804-81), British prime minister, on rival
prime minister William Ewart Gladstone (1809-98)

The manners of a cad and the tongue of a bargee.

Herbert Asquith (1852-1928), British prime minister, on Joseph
Chamberlain (1836-1914), British politician

Listening to a speech by Chamberlain is like paying a visit to Woolworth's; everything in its place and nothing above sixpence.

Aneurin Bevan (1897-1960) on Neville Chamberlain (1869-1940)

What other man within the walls of parliament, however hasty, rude and petulant, hath exhibited such manifold instances of bad manners, bad feelings, bad reasonings, bad language and bad law?

Walter Savage Landor (1775-1864), British poet, on Henry Peter Brougham (1778-1868), British statesman and author

He would kill his own mother just so that he could use her skin to make a drum to beat his own praises.

Margot Asquith (1864-1945), writer and wife of Prime Minister Herbert Henry Asquith, on Winston Churchill (1874-1965)

A retail mind in a wholesale business.

David Lloyd George (1863-1945) on Neville Chamberlain (1869-1940)

Winston has devoted the best years of his life to preparing his impromptu speeches.

F. E. Smith (1872-1930) on Winston Churchill (1874-1965)

Dear Randolph, utterly unspoilt by failure.

Noël Coward (1899-1973) on Randolph Churchill (1849-95)

He occasionally stumbled over the truth, but hastily picked himself up and hurried on as if nothing had happened.

Winston Churchill on Stanley Baldwin (1867-1947)

I met Curzon in Downing Street, from whom I got the sort of greeting a corpse would give to an undertaker.

attr. Stanley Baldwin on Lord Curzon (1859-1925)

His idea of getting hold of the right end of the stick is to snatch it from the hands of somebody who is using it effectively, and to hit him over the head with it.

George Bernard Shaw (1856-1950), Irish playwright, on Theodore Roosevelt (1858-1919), 26th American president

He objected to ideas only when others had them.

A. J. P. Taylor, British historian, on Ernest Bevin (1881-1951) British politician

Reader, suppose you were an idiot; and suppose you were a member of Congress; but I repeat myself.

Mark Twain (1835-1910), American writer, on Congress

You've no idea what it costs to keep the old man in poverty.

Lord Louis Mountbatten (1900-79) on Mahatma Gandhi (1869-1948)

As he rose like a rocket, he fell like a stick.

Thomas Paine (1737-1809), British political philosopher, on
Edmund Burke (1729-97), British author and statesman

He slept more than any other president,
whether by day or night. Nero fiddled, but
Coolidge only snored.

H. L. Mencken (1880-1956) on Calvin Coolidge (1872-1933)

I am sir, for the last time in my life,
Your Humble Servant Horace Walpole.

Horace Walpole (1717-97), British prime minister, ending a letter
to an uncle with whom he had quarrelled

As an intellectual he bestowed upon the games of golf and bridge all the enthusiasm and perseverance that he withheld from books and ideas.

Emmet Hughes, American writer, on Dwight Eisenhower (1890-1969), 34th American president

He couldn't see a belt without hitting below it.

Margot Asquith (1864-1945) on David Lloyd George (1863-1945), British prime minister

... only a frantic pair of moustaches.

T. E. Lawrence (1888-1935) on Ferdinand Foch (1851-1929), French marshal

The Right Honourable Gentleman is indebted to his memory for his jests and to his imagination for his facts.

Richard Brinsley Sheridan (1751-1816), Irish playwright and politician, on Henry Dundas (1742-1811), British politician

He brings to the fierce struggle of politics the tepid enthusiasm of a lazy summer afternoon at a cricket match.

Aneurin Bevan (1897-1960) on Clement Attlee (1883-1967), British prime minister

Chamberlain is no better than a Mayor of Birmingham, and in a lean year at that.

Lord Hugh Cecil on Neville Chamberlain (1869-1940)

He thinks himself deaf because he no longer hears himself talked of.

Charles Maurice de Talleyrand-Périgord (1754-1838) on Vicomte de Chateaubriand (1768-1848)

Garfield has shown that he is not possessed of the backbone of an angleworm.

Ulysses S. Grant (1822-85), 18th American president, on James A. Garfield (1831-81), 20th American president

The people are tired of a man who has not an idea above a horse or a cigar.

Joseph Brown on Ulysses S. Grant, 18th American president

He writes the worst English that I have ever encountered. It reminds me of a string of wet sponges; it reminds me of tattered washing on the line; it reminds me of stale bean soup, of college yells, of dogs barking idiotically through endless nights. It is so bad that a sort of grandeur creeps into it. It drags itself out of the dark abysm of pish and crawls insanely up the topmost pinnacle of posh. It is rumble and bumble. It is flap and doodle. It is balder and dash.

H. L. Mencken (1880-1956), American journalist and critic, on Warren G. Harding (1865-1923), American president

He's thin, boys. He's thin as piss on a hot rock.

Senator William E. Jenner on W. Averell Harriman (1891-1986), governor of New York

He did not seem to care which way he
travelled, as long as he was in the driver's seat.

Lord Beaverbrook (1879-1964) on David Lloyd George (1863-1945)

The moral character of Jefferson was
repulsive. Continually puling about liberty,
equality, and the degrading curse of slavery,
he brought his own children to the hammer,
and made money of his debaucheries.

Alexander Hamilton (1757-1804), American politician, on
Thomas Jefferson (1743-1826), 3rd American president

I think of Mr Stevenson as a consumptive youth weaving garlands of sad flowers with pale, weak hands.

George Moore (1852-1933) on Robert Louis Stevenson (1850-94)

He has a gross and repulsive face but appears *bon enfant* when you talk to him. But he is the dullest Briton of them all.

Henry James (1843-1916) on Anthony Trollope (1815-82)

❮on writers❯

I doubt that the infant monster has any more to give.

Henry James on Rudyard Kipling (1865-1936)

A hack writer who would not have been considered a fourth rate in Europe, who tricked out a few of the old proven 'sure-fire' literary skeletons with sufficient local colour to intrigue the superficial and the lazy.

William Faulkner (1897-1962) on Mark Twain (1835-1910)

To me Pound remains the exquisite showman minus the show.

Ben Hecht on Ezra Pound (1885-1972)

Literature cannot be the business of a woman's life, because of the sacredness of her duties at home.

Robert Southey (1774-1843) on Charlotte Brontë (1816-55)

One of the surest signs of his genius is that women dislike his books.

George Orwell (1903-50) on Joseph Conrad (1857-1924)

One could always baffle Conrad by saying 'humour'.

H. G. Wells (1866-1946) on Joseph Conrad

Tell me, when you're alone with Max, does he take off his face and reveal his mask?

Oscar Wilde (1854-1900) on Max Beerbohm (1872-1956)

He is the bully on the Left Bank, always ready to twist the milksop's arm.

Cyril Connolly (1903-74) on Ernest Hemingway (1899-1961)

Never have I read such tosh. As for the first two chapters, we will let them pass, but the third, the fourth the fifth the sixth – merely the scratchings of pimples on the body of the boot-boy at Claridges.

Virginia Woolf (1882-1941) on James Joyce's *Ulysses*

We have met too late. You are too old for me to have any effect on you.

James Joyce (1882-1941) to W. B. Yeats (1865-1939)

Obsessed with self. Dead eyes and a red beard, long narrow face. A strange bird.

John Galsworthy (1867-1933) on D. H. Lawrence (1885-1930)

Books seem to me to be pestilent things, and infect all that trade in them ... with something very perverse and brutal. Printers, binders, sellers and others that make a trade and gain out of them, have universally so odd a turn and corruption of mind that they have a way of dealing peculiar to themselves and not conform to the good of society and that general fairness which cements mankind.

John Locke (1632-1704), British philosopher

Bennett – sort of a pig in clover.

D. H. Lawrence (1885-1930) on Arnold Bennett (1867-1931), British novelist

I have discovered that our great favourite, Miss Austen, is my countrywoman ... with whom mamma before her marriage was acquainted. Mamma says that she was then the prettiest, silliest, most affected husband hunting butterfly she ever remembers.

Mary Russell Mitford, letter to Sir William Elford (3 April 1815), on Jane Austen (1775-1817)

One of the most extraordinary successes in the history of civilisation was achieved by an idler, a lecher, a drunkard, and a snob, nor was this success of that sudden explosive kind. It was the supreme expression of an entire life.

Lytton Strachey (1880-1932) on James Boswell (1740-95), British author and biographer

Sitting in a sewer and adding to it.

Thomas Carlyle (1795-1881), Scottish historian and essayist, on Algernon Charles Swinburne (1837-1909), British poet

I hate the whole race of them, there never existed a more worthless set than Byron and his friends.

Duke of Wellington (1769-1852) on Lord Byron (1788-1824)

He grew up from manhood into boyhood.

R. A. Knox (1888-1957) on G. K. Chesterton (1874-1936)

Coleridge was a muddle-headed metaphysician who by some strange streak of fortune turned out a few poems amongst the dreary flood of inanity that was his wont.

William Morris (1834-96) on Samuel Taylor Coleridge (1772-1834)

He has plenty of music in him, but he cannot get it out.

Alfred, Lord Tennyson (1809-92) on Robert Browning (1812-89)

... a flabby lemon and pink giant, who hung his mouth open as though he were an animal at the zoo inviting buns – especially when the ladies were present.

Wyndham Lewis (1882-1957) on Ford Madox Ford (1873-1939)

I wish her characters would talk a little less like the heroes and heroines of police reports.

George Eliot on Charlotte Brontë's *Jane Eyre*

All the faults of *Jane Eyre* are magnified thousandfold and the only consolation which we have in reflecting upon it, is that it will never be generally read.

James Lorimer, British critic, on Emily Brontë's *Wuthering Heights*

Mrs Browning's death is rather a relief to me, I must say. No more Aurora Leighs, thank God!

Edward Fitzgerald, British poet, on Elizabeth Barrett Browning (1806-61)

A fungus of pendulous shape.

Alice James on George Eliot (1819-80)

The very pimple of the age's humbug.

Nathaniel Hawthorne (1804-64), US writer, on Edward Bulwer-Lytton (1803-73), British dandy and novelist

I wonder that he is not thrashed; but his littleness is his protection, no man shoots a wren.

William Broome on Alexander Pope (1688-1744)

A village explainer. Excellent if you were a village, but if you were not, not.

Gertrude Stein (1874-1946) on Ezra Pound (1885-1972)

A fat flabby little person with the face of a baker, the clothes of a cobbler, the size of a barrelmaker, the manners of a stocking salesman and the dress of an innkeeper.

Victor de Balabin on Honoré de Balzac (1799-1850)

... a gap-toothed and hoary ape, who now in his dotage spits and chatters from a dirtier perch of his own finding, and fouling; coryphaeus or choragus of his Bulgarian tribe of autocoprophagaus baboons.

Algernon Charles Swinburne (1837-1909) on Ralph Waldo Emerson (1803-82)

⌐on writers⌐

If he hides in a quarry he puts reds flags all round

George Bernard Shaw (1856-1950) on T. E. Lawrence (1888-1935), writer and adventurer

He's impossible. He's pathetic and preposterous. He writes like a sick man.

Gertrude Stein (1874-1946) on D. H. Lawrence (1885-1930)

Reading him is like wading through glue.

Alfred, Lord Tennyson (1809-92) on Ben Jonson (1572-1637)

So grave, sententious, dogmatical a Rogue, that there is no enduring him.

Jonathan Swift (1667-1745), satirist and writer, on Daniel Defoe (1660-1731)

A totally disinherited waif.

George Santayana (1863-1952), American philosopher, on Charles Dickens (1812-70)

He has never played any significant part in any movement more significant than that of a fly... on a wheel.

Saturday Review (1857) on Charles Dickens

Of Dicken's style it is impossible to speak in praise. It is jerky, ungrammatical and created by himself in defiance of rules... No young novelist should ever dare to imitate the style of Dickens.

Anthony Trollope (1815-82), British novelist, on Charles Dickens in his *Autobiography* (1883)

George Eliot had the heart of Sappho; but the face, with the long proboscis, the protruding teeth of the Apocalyptic horse, betrayed animality.

George Meredith (1828-1909), British novelist and poet, on George Eliot (1819-1880), British novelist

Mr Eliot is at times an excellent poet and has arrived at the supreme Eminence among English critics largely through disguising himself as a corpse.

Ezra Pound (1885-1972) on T. S. Eliot (1888-1965)

Pale, marmoreal Eliot was there last week, like a chapped office boy on a high stool, with a cold in his head.

Virginia Woolf (1882-1941) on T. S. Eliot

Henry James has a mind – a sensibility – so fine that no mere idea could ever penetrate it.

T. S. Eliot on Henry James (1843-1916)

❮on writers❯

Emerson's writing has a cold, cheerless glitter, like the new furniture in a warehouse, which will come of use by and by.

Alexander Smith, American writer, in *Dreamthorp* (1864), on Ralph Waldo Emerson (1803-1882), American essayist and poet

One of the seven humbugs of Xtiandom.

William Morris (1834-96), British designer and writer, on Ralph Waldo Emerson (1803-1882), American essayist and poet

There are two ways of disliking poetry; one way is to dislike it, the other is to read Pope.

Oscar Wilde (1854-1900) on Alexander Pope (1688-1744)

His manners are ninety-nine in a hundred singularly repulsive.

Samuel Taylor Coleridge (1772-1834) on William Hazlitt (1778-1830), British essayist

An unattractive man with an apple-green complexion.

Steven Runciman, British historian, on André Gide (1869-1951), French writer

Hardy became a sort of village atheist brooding and blaspheming over the village idiot.

G. K. Chesterton (1874-1936), British writer, on Thomas Hardy (1840-1928), novelist and poet

All raw, uncooked, protesting.

Virginia Woolf (1882-1941) on Aldous Huxley (1894-1963)

No one has written worse English than Mr Hardy in some of his novels – cumbrous, stilted, ugly and inexpressive – yes.

Virginia Woolf (1882-1941) on
Thomas Hardy (1840-1928)

He is not a proper person to be admitted into respectable society, being the most perverse and malevolent creature that ill-luck has thrown my way.

William Wordsworth (1770-1850),
poet, on William Hazlitt (1778-1830),
British essayist

Without being intentionally obscene, he is thoroughly filthy, and has not the slightest sense of decency. In an old writer, and especially one of that age, I never saw so large a proportion of what may truly be called either trash or ordure.

Robert Southey (1774-1843), poet laureate, in *Commonplace Book* (1812), on Robert Herrick (1592-1674), English poet

The stupid person's idea of the clever person.

Elizabeth Bowen (1899-1973), British writer, in the *Spectator* (1936) on Aldous Huxley (1894-1963), writer

❲on writers❳

One of the nicest old ladies I ever met.

William Faulkner (1897-1962) on Henry James (1843-1916)

Mr Kipling ... stands for everything in this cankered world which I would wish were otherwise.

Dylan Thomas (1914-53), Welsh poet, on Rudyard Kipling (1865-1936)

Mr Lawrence looked like a plaster gnome on a stone toadstool in some suburban garden ... he looked as if he had just returned from spending an uncomfortable night in a very dark cave.

Dame Edith Sitwell (1887-1964), British author and poet, on D. H. Lawrence (1885-1930)

Crude, immoral, vulgar and senseless.

Leo Tolstoy (1828-1910) on William Shakespeare (1564-1616)

Shakespeare – what trash are his works in the gross.

Edward Young, British poet, in 1820

To think of him dribbling his powerful intellect through the gimlet holes of poetry.

Thomas Carlyle (1795-1881) on Alfred, Lord Tennyson (1809-92)

His mind is so vile a mind, so cosy, hypocritical, praise-mad, canting, envious, concupiscent.

Samuel Taylor Coleridge (1772-1834), British poet, on Samuel Richardson (1689-1761), British novelist

Sir, he was dull in company, dull in his closet, dull everywhere. He was dull in a new way and that made people think him great.

Samuel Johnson (1709-84) on Thomas Gray (1716-71), British poet

Those base, servile, self-degraded wretches, Virgil and Horace.

William Cobbett (1763-1835) on the Classical poets Virgil (70-19 BC) and Horace (65-8 BC)

Virginia Woolf's writing is no more than glamorous knitting. I believe she must have a pattern somewhere.

Dame Edith Sitwell (1887-1964) on Virginia Woolf (1882-1941)

I'm sure the poor woman meant well, but I wish she'd stick to recreating the glory that was Greece and not muck about with dear old modern homos.

Noël Coward (1899-1973) on Mary Renault, known for her historical fiction about Ancient Greece

An animated adenoid.

Norman Douglas (1868-1952),
English novelist, on Ford Madox
Ford (1873-1939)

A lewd vegetarian.

Charles Kingsley (1819-75)
on Percy Bysshe Shelley
(1792-1822)

An idiot child
screaming in a
hospital.

H. G. Wells (1866-1946) on George Bernard Shaw (1856-1950)

Filth. Nothing but obscenities.

Joseph Conrad (1857-1924) on D.H. Lawrence (1885-1930)

Owen's tiny corpus is perhaps the most over-rated poetry in the twentieth century.

Craig Raine, British poet, on Wilfred Owen (1893-1918), British poet

We invite people like that to tea, but we don't marry them.

Lady Chetwode on her future son-in-law, John Betjeman (1906-84)

Living almost always among intellectuals, she preserved to the age of fifty-six that contempt for ideas which is normal among boys and girls of fifteen.

Odell Sheperd, American writer, on Louisa May Alcott (1832-88)

T. S. Eliot and I like to play, but I like to play Euchre, while he likes to play Eucharist.

Robert Frost (1874-1963) on T. S. Eliot (1888-1965)

His imagination resembles the wings of an ostrich.

Thomas Babington Macaulay (1800-59) on John Dryden (1631-1700), English poet

He has the most remarkable and seductive genius – and I should say about the smallest in the world.

Lytton Strachey (1880-1932), British writer, on Max Beerbohm (1872-1956), author and cartoonist

What is Conrad but the wreck of Stevenson floating about in the slipsop of Henry James?

George Moore (1852-1933)
on Joseph Conrad (1857-1924)

His verse... is the beads without the string.

Gerard Manley Hopkins (1844-89) on Robert Browning (1812-89)

... a sort of gutless Kipling.

George Orwell (1903-50)
on W. H. Auden (1907-73)

The cynic parasite.

Benjamin Disraeli (1804-81) on William Makepeace Thackeray (1811-63)

... a tub of old guts.

Ezra Pound (1885-1972) on Gertrude Stein (1874-1946)

A hyena that wrote poetry on tombs.

Friedrich Nietzsche (1844-1900) on Dante Alighieri (1265-1321)

A monster, gibbering, shrieking and gnashing imprecations against mankind.

William Makepeace Thackeray on Jonathan Swift (1667-1745)

What an old covered wagon she is.

F. Scott Fitzgerald (1896-1940) on Gertrude Stein (1874-1946)

A tadpole of the lakes.

Lord Byron (1788-1824) on John Keats (1795-1821)

With the single exception of Homer, there is no eminent writer, not even Sir Walter Scott, whom I can despise so entirely as I despise Shakespeare when I measure my mind against his... it would positively be a relief to me to dig him up and throw stones at him.

George Bernard Shaw (1856-1950) on William Shakespeare (1564-1616)

He is all blood, dirt and sucked sugar stick.

W. B. Yeats (1865-1939) on Wilfred Owen (1893-1918)

She looked like Lady Chatterley above the waist and the gamekeeper below.

Cyril Connolly (1903-74), on Vita Sackville-West (1892-1962)

He is all ice and woodenfaced acrobatics.

Wyndham Lewis (1882-1957) on W. H. Auden (1907-73)

I want words sufficient to express thy viperous Treason... there never lived a viler viper on the face of the earth than thou.

Sir Edward Coke (1552-1634) to Sir Walter Raleigh (1552-1618), Elizabethan writer, courtier and explorer

A dirty man with opium-glazed eyes and rat-taily hair.

Lady Frederick Cavendish, British aristocrat, on Alfred, Lord Tennyson (1809-92)

A man carved from a turnip looking out from astonished eyes.

W. B. Yeats on George Moore
(1852-1933), Anglo-Irish novelist

This enormous dunghill.

Voltaire (1694-1778) on William Shakespeare (1564-1616)

The godless arch scoundrel Voltaire is dead – dead like a dog, like a beast.

Wolfgang Amadeus Mozart (1756-91)

A great cow full of ink.

Gustave Flaubert (1821-80) on George Sand (1804-76)

Thackeray settled like a meat-fly on whatever one had got for dinner; and made one sick of it.

John Ruskin (1819-1900) on William Makepeace Thackeray (1811-63), British novelist and critic

A reptile marking his path wherever he goes and breathing a mildew at everything fresh and fragrant; a midnight ghoul preying on rottenness and repulsive filth. A creature hated by his nearest intimates and bearing his consciousness thereof upon his distorted features and upon his despicable soul.

Walt Whitman (1819-91) on James Gordon Bennett, editor and journalist of the *New York Herald*

The enemy of all mankind, you are, full of the lust of enmity. It is not the hatred of falsehood which inspires you. It is the hatred of people, of flesh and blood. It is a perverted blood lust, why don't you own it?

D. H. Lawrence (1885-1930) on Bertrand Russell (1872-1970)

He is the old maid among novelists.

Dame Rebecca West (1892-1983) on H. G. Wells (1866-1946)

Is Wordsworth a bell with a wooden tongue?

Ralph Waldo Emerson (1803-82) on William Wordsworth (1770-1850)

Jane Austen's books, too are absent from this library. Just that one omission alone would make a fairly good library out of a library that hadn't a book in it.

Mark Twain (1835-1910) on Jane Austen (1775-1817)

A large shaggy dog just unchained scouring the beaches of the world and baying at the moon.

Robert Louis Stevenson (1850-94) on Walt Whitman (1819-91)

The death of a member of the lower classes could be trusted to give him a good chuckle.

W. Somerset Maugham (1874-1965) on Henry James (1843-1916)

A cliché-ridden humbug and pie-fingering hack.

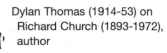

Dylan Thomas (1914-53) on Richard Church (1893-1972), author

I cannot abide Conrad's souvenir shop style and bottled ships and shell necklaces of romanticist clichés.

Vladimir Nabokov (1899-1977) on Joseph Conrad (1857-1924)

Chaucer, notwithstanding the praises bestowed upon him, I think obscene and contemptible; he owes his celebrity merely to his antiquity.

Lord Byron (1788-1824) on Geoffrey Chaucer (c.1345-1400)

A huge pendulum attached to a small clock.

Ivan Panin, Russian critic, on Samuel Taylor Coleridge (1772-1834), poet

The undisputed fame enjoyed by Shakespeare as a writer... is, like every other lie, a great evil.

Leo Tolstoy (1828-1910) on William Shakespeare (1564-1616)

Why sir, Sherry is dull, naturally dull; but it must have taken him a great deal of pains to become what we now see him. Such excess of stupidity, sir, is not in nature.

Samuel Johnson (1709-84) on Thomas Sheridan (1719-88)

I am fairly unrepentant about her poetry. I really think that three quarters of it is gibberish. However, I must crush down these thoughts, otherwise the dove of peace will shit on me.

Noël Coward (1899-1973) on Dame Edith Sitwell (1887-1964)

A poor creature, who has said or done nothing worth a serious man taking the trouble of remembering.

Thomas Carlyle (1795-1881) on Percy Bysshe Shelley (1792-1822)

To see him fumbling with our rich and delicate English is like seeing a Sèvres vase in the hands of a chimpanzee.

Evelyn Waugh (1903-66) on Stephen Spender (1909-95)

Dean Swift, by his lordship's own account, was so intoxicated with the love of flattery, he sought it amongst the lowest of people and the silliest of women; and was never so well pleased with any companions as those that worshipped him, while he insulted them.

Lady Mary Wortley Montagu (1689-1762) on Jonathan Swift (1667-1745)

Conrad spent a day finding the *mot juste*: then killed it.

Ford Madox Ford (1873-1939) on Joseph Conrad (1857-1924)

Not quite Milton, a sort of origami Milton, the paper phoenix fluttering in the wizard's hand.

Hugh Kenner on Wallace Stevens (1879-1955), American poet

Jo Davies goes wobbling with his arse out behind as though he were about to make everyone he meets a wall to piss against.

John Manningham, English diarist, on Sir John Davies (1569-1626), English poet and attorney-general

To the King's theatre, where we saw *A Midsummer Night's Dream*, which I had never seen before, nor shall ever again, for it is the most insipid, ridiculous play that I ever saw in my life.

Samuel Pepys (1633-1703), English diarist, on William Shakespeare (1564-1616)

The first man to have cut a swathe through the theatre and left it strewn with virgins.

Frank Harris (1856-1931), English author and journalist, on George Bernard Shaw

He seems to me the most vulgar-minded genius that ever produced a great effect in literature.

George Eliot (1819-80), British novelist, on Lord Byron

Gertrude Stein's prose is a cold, black suet-pudding. We can represent it as a cold suet-roll of fabulously reptilian length. Cut it at any point, it is... the same heavy, sticky, opaque mass all through, and all along.

Wyndham Lewis (1882-1957) on Gertrude Stein (1874-1946)

I loathe you. You revolt me stewing in your consumption... the Italians were quite right to have nothing to do with you. You are a loathsome reptile – I hope you die.

D. H. Lawrence (1885-1930) to Katherine Mansfield (1888-1923), New Zealand author

He had not the intellectual equipment of a supreme modern poet; except for his genius he was an ordinary nineteenth-century gentleman, with little culture and no ideas.

Matthew Arnold (1822-88), British poet and critic, on Lord Byron (1788-1824)

A coxcomb who would have gone into hysterics if a tailor had laughed at him.

Ebenezer Elliott (1781-1849), British poet and steel founder, on Lord Byron

Mad, bad and dangerous to know.

Lady Caroline Lamb (1785-1828), British aristocrat and writer, on Lord Byron

The world is rid of Lord Byron, but the deadly slime of his touch still remains.

John Constable (1776-1837), artist, on Lord Byron's' death

The most affected of sensualists and the most pretentious of profligates.

Algernon Charles Swinburne (1837-1909), poet, on Lord Byron

The language of Aristophanes reeks of his miserable quackery: it is made up of the lowest and most miserable puns; he doesn't even please the people, and to men of judgement and honour he is intolerable; his arrogance is insufferable, and all honest men detest his malice.

Plutarch (c. 46-c.120), Greek biographer and moralist, on Aristophanes (c. 448-c. 388 BC), Greek playwright.

Poor Matt. He's gone to heaven, no doubt, but he won't like God.

Robert Louis Stevenson (1850-94) on Matthew Arnold

Freud Madox Fraud

Osbert Sitwell (1892-1969), British writer, on Ford Madox Ford (1873-1939), British writer

E. M. Forster never gets any further than warming the teapot. He's a rare fine hand at that. Feel this teapot. Is it not beautifully warm? Yes, but there ain't going to be no tea.

Katherine Mansfield (1888-1923), on E. M. Forster (1879-1970), British novelist, in her *Journal* (1917)

He is a mediocre man – and knows it, or suspects it, which is worse; he will come to no good, and in the meantime he's treated rudely by waiters and is not really admired even by the middle-class dowagers.

Lytton Strachey (1880-1932), British writer, on E. M. Forster

He is limp and milder than the breath of a cow.

Virginia Woolf (1882-1941), on E .M. Forster

Of Byron one can say, as of no other English poet of his eminence, that he added nothing to the language, that he discovered nothing in the sounds, and developed nothing in the meaning, of individual words.

T. S. Eliot (1888-1965) on Lord Byron
(1788-1824)

This awful Whitman. This post-mortem poet. This poet with the private soul leaking out of him all the time. All his privacy leaking out in a sort of dribble, oozing into the universe.

D. H. Lawrence (1885-1930) on Walt Whitman (1819-91),
American poet

Some call Pope little nightingale – all sound and no sense.

Lady Mary Wortley Montagu (1689-1762) on Alexander Pope
(1688-1744)

Monsieur Zola is determined to show that if he has not genius he can at least be dull.

Oscar Wilde (1854-1900) on Emile Zola (1840-1902)

The jingle man.

Ralph Waldo Emerson (1803-82) on Edgar Allan Poe (1809-49)

I invariably miss most of the lines in the last act of an Ibsen play; I always have my fingers in my ears, waiting for the loud report that means that the heroine has just Passed On.

Dorothy Parker (1893-1967) on Henrik Ibsen (1828-1906)

... bent on groping for horror by night, and blinking like a stupid old owl when the warm sunlight of the best of life dances into his wrinkled eyes.

The Gentlewoman magazine on Henrik Ibsen

Henry James had turned his back on one of the great events in the world's history, the rise of the United States, in order to report tittle-tattle at tea parties in English country houses.

W. Somerset Maugham (1874-1965) on Henry James

I detest the country. Yeats will amuse me
part of the time and bore me to death with
psychical research the rest. I regard the visit
as a duty to posterity.

Ezra Pound (1885-1972), American poet, on visiting
William Butler Yeats (1865-1939), Irish poet

[A book by Henry James] is like a church lit
but without a congregation to distract you,
with every light and line focused on the
high altar. And on the altar, very reverently
placed, intensely there, is a dead kitten, an
eggshell, a bit of string.

H. G. Wells (1866-1946) on Henry James (1843-1916)

... stewed-up fragments of quotation in the
sauce of a would-be dirty mind.

D. H. Lawrence (1885-1930) on James Joyce (1882-1941)

I don't think I have ever seen a nastier
looking man. Some people show evil as a
great racehorse shows breeding. They have
the dignity of a hard chancre. Lewis did not
show evil; he just looked nasty.

Ernest Hemingway (1899-1961) on Wyndham Lewis
(1882-1957)

Byron can only bore the spleen.

Charles Lamb (1775-1834) on Lord Byron

❮on writers❯

He is blatant, full of foolish archaisms, obscure through awkward language, not subtle thought, and formless.

Rupert Brooke (1887-1915) on Ezra Pound (1885-1972)

I believe he creates a milieu in which art is impossible.

Ezra Pound on G. K. Chesterton (1874-1936)

Nothing but a pack of lies.

Damon Runyon (1884-1946) on *Alice in Wonderland* by Lewis Carroll (1832-98)

From the moment I picked up your book until I laid it down I was convulsed with laughter. Someday I intend reading it.

Groucho Marx (1895-1977) on *Dawn Ginsbergh's Revenge* by Sydney J. Perelman

I fell asleep reading a dull book, and I dreamed that I was reading on, so I awoke from sheer boredom.

Heinrich Heine (1797-1856)

A Methodist parson in Bedlam.

Horace Walpole (1717-97) on Dante (1265-1321)

Here are Johnny Keats' piss-a-bed poetry, and three novels by God knows whom ... No more Keats, I entreat: flay him alive; if some of you don't I must skin him myself: there is no bearing the drivelling idiotism of the Mankin.

Lord Byron (1788-1824) on John Keats (1795-1821)

The kind of man that Keats was gets ever more horrible to me. Force of hunger for pleasure of every kind, and want of all other force – such a soul, it would once have been very evident, was a chosen vessel of Hell.

Thomas Carlyle (1795-1881) on John Keats

Byron! – he would be all forgotten today if he had lived to be a florid old gentleman with iron-grey whiskers, writing very long, very able letters to *The Times* about the repeal of corn laws.

Max Beerbohm (1872-1956) on Lord Byron (1788-1824)

An unmanly sort of man whose love-life seems to have been largely confined to crying in laps and playing mouse.

W. H. Auden (1907-73) on Edgar Allan Poe (1809-49)

Of all bitches alive or dead, a scribbling woman is the most canine.

Lord Byron on Anna Seward (1747-1809)

Walt Whitman is as unacquainted with art as a hog with mathematics.

London Critic on Walt Whitman (1819-91)

Longfellow is to poetry what the barrel-organ is to music.

Van Wyck Brooks, American critic,
on Henry Wadsworth Longfellow (1807-82)

Waldo is one of those people who would be enormously improved by death.

Saki (H. H. Munro) (1870-1916) on Ralph Waldo Emerson (1803-82)

Carlyle is a poet to whom nature has denied the faculty of verse.

Alfred, Lord Tennyson (1809-92) on Thomas Carlyle (1795-1881)

We can say of Shakespeare , that never has a man turned so little knowledge to such great account.

T. S. Eliot (1888-1965) on William Shakespeare (1564-1616)

I have tried lately to read Shakespeare, and found it so intolerably dull that it nauseated me.

Charles Darwin (1809-82) on William Shakespeare

A strange horrible business, but I suppose good enough for Shakespeare's day.

Queen Victoria (1819-1901) on Shakespeare's *King Lear*

It is not surprising to learn that Marlowe was stabbed in a tavern brawl: what would be utterly unbelievable would be his having succeeded in stabbing anyone else.

George Bernard Shaw on Christopher Marlowe (1564-93)

George too Shaw to be Good.

Dylan Thomas (1914-53) on George Bernard Shaw (1856-1950)

Poor Shelley always was, and is, a kind of ghastly object; colourless, pallid, tuneless, without health or warmth or vigour.

Thomas Carlyle (1795-1881) on Percy Bysshe Shelley (1792-1822)

on writers

I really enjoy his stage directions... He uses the English language like a truncheon.

Max Beerbohm (1872-1956) on George Bernard Shaw

Mr Shaw is (I suspect) the only man on earth who has never written poetry.

G. K. Chesterton (1874-1936) on George Bernard Shaw

Isn't she a poisonous thing of a woman, lying, concealing, flipping, plagiarising, misquoting and being as clever a crooked literary publicist as ever.

Dylan Thomas (1914-53) on Dame Edith Sitwell

Then Edith Sitwell appeared, her nose longer than an ant-eater's, and read some of her absurd stuff.

Lytton Strachey (1880-1932) on Dame Edith Sitwell (1887-1964)

Steele might become a reasonably good writer if he would pay a little attention to grammar, learn something about the propriety and disposition of words and, incidentally, get some information on the subject he intends to handle.

Jonathan Swift (1667-1745) on Richard Steele (1672-1729)

... a perpetual functioning of genius without truth, feeling, or any adequate matter to be functioning on.

Gerard Manley Hopkins (1844-89) on Algernon Swinburne (1837-1909)

Let simple Wordsworth chime his childish verse, and brother Coleridge lull the babe at nurse.

Lord Byron (1788-1824)

Everything which another man would have hidden, everything the publication of which would have made another man hang himself, was a matter of exaltation to his weak and diseased mind.

Thomas Babington Macaulay (1800-59), British historian, on James Boswell (1740-95), author and biographer

A vain silly, transparent coxcomb without either solid talents or a solid nature.

J. G. Lockhart (1794-1854), Scottish writer, on Samuel Pepys (1633-1703), diarist

A good man fallen among Fabians.

attr. Vladimir Ilyich Lenin (1870-1924) on George Bernard Shaw (1874-1936)

He walked as if he had fouled his small clothes and looks as if he smelt it.

Christopher Smart (1722-71), British poet on Thomas Gray (1716-71), British poet

You can gain nothing by reading her. It is like eating snowballs, with which one can surfeit one's self without satisfying the stomach.

Napoleon Bonaparte (1769-1821) on Madame Marie de Sévigné (1626-96)

There is no arguing with Johnson; for when his pistol misses fire, he knocks you down with the butt end of it.

Oliver Goldsmith (1728-74), British poet, on Samuel Johnson (1709-84)

In George Meredith there is nothing but crackjaw sentences, empty and unpleasant in the mouth as sterile nuts.

George Moore (1852-1933) on George Meredith (1828-1909)

A great author, notwithstanding his *Dictionary* is imperfect, his *Rambler* pompous, his *Idler* inane, his *Lives* unjust, his poetry inconsiderable, his learning common, his ideas vulgar, his *Irene* a child of mediocrity, his genius and wit moderate, his precepts wordly, his politics narrow and his religion bigoted.

Robert Potter, British critic, on Samuel Johnson, in 1781

I should never write on him as I detest him too much ever to trust myself as a critic of him.

Ezra Pound (1885-1972) on George Meredith (1828-1909)

Vain Nashe, railing Nashe, cracking Nashe, bibbing Nashe, swaddish Nashe, roguish Nashe... the swish-swash of the press, the bum of impudency, the shambles of beastliness.

Gabriel Harvey (c.1550-1631), scholar and writer, on Thomas Nashe (1567-1601), English playwright

This dodipoule, this didopper... Why, thou arrant butter whore, thou cotqueane & scrattop of scoldes, with thou never leave afflicting a dead Carcasse... a wispe, a wispe, rippe, rippe, you kitchin-stuff wrangler!

Thomas Nashe on Gabriel Harvey

Dear Sam,
I shall take your advice and not read your
book. It would probably pain me and not
benefit you.
Your Affectionate father,
T. Butler

Canon T. Butler to his son, Samuel Butler (1835-1902)

It is long, yet
vigorous, like the penis
of a jackass.

Revd Sydney Smith (1771-1845) on
the writings of Henry Peter Brougham
(1778-1868)

Dank, limber verses,
stuft with lakeside
sedges, And propt with
rotten stakes from
rotten hedges.

Walter Savage Landor (1775-1864), British poet, on
William Wordsworth (1770-1850)

Mr Wordsworth, a stupid man, with a
decided gift for portraying nature in
vignettes, never ruined anyone's morals,
unless, perhaps, he has driven some
susceptible persons to crime in a very fury
of boredom.

Ezra Pound (1885-1972) on William Wordsworth

A blatant Bassarid of Boston, a rampant Maenad of Massachusetts.

Algernon Charles Swinburne (1837-1909) on Harriet Beecher Stowe (1811-96), humanitarian and novelist

Open him at any page: and there lies the English language not, as George Moore said of Pater, in a glass coffin, but in a large, sultry and unhygienic box.

Dylan Thomas (1914-53) on William Wordsworth (1770-1850)

Anyone who has seen Saint-Marc Giradin walking the street has been immediately struck by the notion of a big goose, deeply in love with itself, but scuttling over the road in panic to escape from a coach.

Charles Baudelaire (1821-67) on Saint-Marc Giradin, anti-romantic critic and publicist

... our authors are vulgar, gross, illiberal; the theatre swarms with wretched translations, and ballad operas and we have nothing new but improving abuse.

Horace Walpole (1717-97) on his life and time

Tennyson is a beautiful half of a poet.

Ralph Waldo Emerson (1803-82) on Alfred, Lord Tennyson (1809-92)

... there was little about melancholy that he didn't know; there was little else that he did.

W. H. Auden (1907-73) on Alfred, Lord Tennyson

I don't think Robert Browning was very good in bed. His wife probably didn't care for him very much. He snored and had fantasies about twelve-year-old girls.

W. H. Auden on Robert Browning (1812-89)

The way Bernard Shaw believes in himself is very refreshing in these atheistic days when so many people believe in no God at all.

Israel Zangwill (1864-1926) on George Bernard Shaw (1856-1950)

In his endeavours to corrupt my mind he has sought to make me smile first at Vice, saying, 'There is nothing to which a woman may not be reconciled by repetition or familiarity.' There is no vice with which he has not endeavoured in this manner to familiarise me.

Annabella Milbanke, Lady Byron on her husband, Lord Byron

❲on writers❳

He has never been known to use a word that might send a man to a dictionary.

William Faulkner (1897-1962) on Ernest Hemingway (1899-1961)

Poor Faulkner. Does he really think emotions come from big words.

Ernest Hemingway on William Faulkner

He is a system of assumed personas.

H. G. Wells (1866-1946) on Ford Madox Ford (1873-1939)

… a nice, acrid, savage, pathetic old chap.

I. A. Richards (1893-1979) on Robert Frost (1874-1963)

The work of Henry James has always seemed divisible by a simple dynastic arrangement into three reigns: James I, James II and the Old Pretender.

Philip Guedalla (1889-1944), historian and biographer, on Henry James (1843-1916)

❰on writers❱

I have just read a long novel by Henry
James. Much of it made me think of the
priest condemned for a long space to
confess nuns.

William Butler Yeats (1865-1939) on Henry James

I could not write the words Mr Joyce uses:
my prudish hands would refuse to form
the letters.

George Bernard Shaw (1856-1950) on James Joyce (1882-1941)

My God, what a clumsy olla putrida James
Joyce is! Nothing but old fags and cabbage
stumps of quotations from the Bible and the
rest stewed in the juice of deliberate,
journalistic dirty-mindedness.

D. H. Lawrence (1885-1930) on James Joyce

Probably Joyce thinks that because he prints
all the dirty little words he is a great hero.

George Moore (1852-1933) on James Joyce

Kipling is a jingo imperialist, he is morally
insensitive and aesthetically disgusting.

George Orwell (1903-50) on Rudyard Kipling (1865-1936)

... a mercenary, hypochondriacal
flibbertigibbet who doesn't take in one of
the six words addressed to him.

Evelyn Waugh (1903-66) on Beverly Nichols

His very frankness is a falsity.
In fact, it seems false than his
insincerity.

Katherine Mansfield (1888-1923) on
her husband John Middleton Murry
(1889-1957)

He would not blow his
nose without
moralising on the
conditions in the
handkerchief industry.

Cyril Connolly on George Orwell (1903-50)

The Hitler of the book racket.

Percy Wyndham Lewis (1884-1957) on Arnold Bennett (1867-1931)

I don't regard Brecht as a man of iron-grey
purpose and intellect. I think he is a
theatrical whore of the first quality.

Peter Hall (b. 1930) on Bertolt Brecht (1898-1956)

Cibber! write all thy Verses upon Glasses,
The only way to save them from our Arses.

Alexander Pope (1688-1744) on Colley Cibber (1671-1757)

In an old writer, and especially one of that
age, I never saw so large a proportion of
what truly be called either trash or ordure.

Robert Southey (1774-1843), British poet laureate, on
Robert Herrick (1591-1674), English poet

❬on writers❭

Never did I see such apparatus got ready for thinking, and never so little thought. He mounts scaffolding, pulleys, and tackles, gathers all the tools in the neighbourhood with labour, with noise, demonstration, precept, and sets – three bricks.

Thomas Carlyle (1795-1881) on Samuel Taylor Coleridge (1772-1834)

He keeps one eye on a daffodil and the other on a canal share.

Walter Savage Landor (1775-1864) on William Wordsworth (1770-1850)

It is written by a man with a diseased mind and soul so black that he would even obscure the darkness of hell.

Senator Reed Smoot on James Joyce (1882-1941)

His brain is a half-inch layer of champagne poured over a bucket of Methodist near-beer.

Benjamin de Casseres on George Bernard Shaw (1856-1950)

He is a shallow, affected, self-conscious fribble.

Vita Sackville-West (1892-1962) on Max Beerbohm (1872-1939)

Ben Jonson! Not another word about him. It makes my blood boil! I haven't the patience to hear the fellow's name. A pigmy! An upstart! A presumptuous valet who dared to be thought more of than Shakespeare in his day!

Walter Savage Landor (1775-1864), poet and essayist, on Ben Jonson (1576-1637), poet and playwright

Oscar Wilde's talent seems to me to be essentially rootless, something growing in glass on a little water.

George Moore (1852-1933, Anglo-Irish novelist

The great honour of that boast is such
That hornets and mad dogs may boast as much.

Lord Hervey (1696-1743) on Alexander Pope (1688-1744)

Byron dealt chiefly in felt and furbelow, wavy Damascus daggers, and pocket pistols studded with paste.

Walter Savage Landor (1775-1864), poet and essayist, on Lord Byron (1788-1824)

... the poetry has a good deal of staple about it, and will bear handling; but the inner, the conversational and private, has many coarse intractable dangling threads, fit only for the flockbed equipage of grooms.

Walter Savage Landor on William Wordsworth (1770-1850)

I forgive your reviling of me: there's a shovelful of live coals for your head – does it burn? And am, with true affection – does it burn now?
Ever yours,
Charles Dickens

Charles Dickens (1812-70), letter to Walter Savage Landor

Master, mammoth, mumbler.

Robert Lowell (1917-77) on Ford Madox Ford (1873-1939)

The languid way in which he gives you a handful of numb unresponsive fingers...

Thomas Carlyle (1795-1881) on William Wordsworth (1770-1850)

[Looks like] an umbrella left behind at a picnic.

George Moore (1852-1933) on W. B. Yeats (1865-1939)

... a charlatan, a fool, a lunatic or a child.

R. D. Blumenfield, editor of the *Daily Express* on Sir Arthur Conan Doyle (1859-1930)

It is a better thing to be a starved apothecary than a starved poet. So back to the shop, Mr John. Back to plaster, pills and ointment boxes.

J. G. Lockhart in *Blackwood's Magazine* (1818), on John Keats' poetry

Sir Walter Scott, when all is said and done, is an inspired Butler.

William Hazlitt (1778-1830) on Sir Walter Scott (1771-1832)

A desiccated bourgeois... a fossilised chauvinist, a self-satisfied Englishman.

Pravda on George Bernard Shaw (1856-1950)

Trollope! Did anyone bear a name that predicted a style more Trollopy?

George Moore (1852-1933) on Anthony Trollope (1815-82)

That insolent little ruffian, that crapulous lout. When he quitted a sofa, he left behind him a smear. My wife says he even tried to paw her about.

Norman Cameron (1905-53), British poet, on Dylan Thomas (1914-53)

What a tiresome, affected sod.

Noël Coward (1899-1973) on Oscar Wilde (1854-1900)

Lawrence is in a long line of people, beginning with Heraclitus and ending with Hitler, whose ruling motive is hatred derived from megalomania, and I am sorry to see that I was once so far out in estimating him.

Bertrand Russell (1872-1970) on D. H. Lawrence (1885-1930)

With leering Looks, Bull-fac'd and freckl'd fair,
With two left legs, and Judas colour'd Hair,
And frowzy Pores that taint the ambient Air.

John Dryden (1631-1700) on Jacob Tonson, a publisher

A louse in the locks of literature.

Alfred, Lord Tennyson (1809-1892), on critic Churton Collins

This obscure, eccentric and disgusting poem

Voltaire (1694-1778) on Milton's *Paradise Lost*

The verses, when they were written,
resembled nothing so much as spoonfuls
of boiling oil, ladled out by a fiendish
monkey at an upstairs window upon such
of the passers-by whom the wretch had a
grudge against.

Lytton Strachey (1880-1932) on
Alexander Pope (1688-1744)

Yet let me flap this
bug with gilded
wings,

This painted child
of dirt, that stinks
and sings...

Alexander Pope (1688-
1744) on Hervey, John,
Baron Hervey of Ickworth
(1696-1743), British
courtier and writer

... a poor, thin, spasmodic hectic shrill and pallid being.

Thomas Carlyle (1795-1881)
on Percy Bysshe Shelley (1792-1822)

Wordsworth has left a bad impression wherever he visited in town by his egotism, vanity and bigotry.

John Keats (1795-1821) on William Wordsworth

A mere ulcer; a sore from head to foot; a poor devil so completely flayed that there is not a square inch of healthy flesh on his carcass; an overgrown pimple, sore to the touch.

Quarterly Review (1817) on William Hazlitt (1778-1830)

Emerson is one who lives instinctively on ambrosia – and leaves everything indigestible on his plate.

Friedrich Nietszche (1844-1900) on Ralph Waldo Emerson (1803-82)

He is a sort of M. de Sade, but does not write so well.

Edmund Gosse (1849-1928) on James Joyce (1882 1941)

Just for a handful of silver he left us,
Just for a riband to stick in his coat.

Robert Browning (1812-1889) on William Wordsworth (1770-1850)

Stoeber's mind, though that is no name to call it by... turns as unansweringly to the false, the meaningless, the unmetrical, as the needle to the pole.

A. E. Housman (1859-1936) on Elias Stoeber (1719-78), editor of classical texts

What does pain me exceedingly is that you should write so badly. These verses are execrable, and I am shocked that you seem unable to perceive it.

Edmund Gosse to Robert Nichols (1893-1944)

on writers

Paradise Lost is one of the books which the reader admires and lays down, and forgets to take up again. Its perusal is a duty rather than a pleasure.

Samuel Johnson (1709-84) on Milton's *Paradise Lost*

About as credulous as an old goose as one could hope to find out of Gotham.

B. G. Johns in *John Aubrey of Wilts* on John Aubrey (1626-97), English biographer and antiquary

Our language sunk under him.

Joseph Addison (1672-1719) on John Milton (1608-74)

You talk about yourself a great deal. That's why there are no distinctive characters in your writing. Your characters are all alike. You probably don't understand women; you've never depicted one successfully.

Leo Tolstoy (1828-1910) to Maxim Gorky (1868-1936)

Fielding had as much humour perhaps as Addison, but, having no idea of grace, is perpetually disgusting.

Horace Walpole (1717-97) on Henry Fielding (1707-54)

If you imagine a Scotch commercial traveller in a Scotch commercial hotel leaning on the bar and calling the barmaid Dearie, them you will know the keynote of Burns' verse.

A. E. Housman (1859-1936) on Robert Burns (1759-96)

I attempt to describe Mr Swinburne; and lo! the Bacchanal screams, the sterile Dolores sweats, serpents dance, men and women wrench, wriggle and foam in an endless alliteration of heated and meaningless words...

Robert Buchanan (1841-1901) on Algernon Charles Swinburne (1837-1909)

She is stupid, heavy and garrulous. Her ideas on morals have the same depth of judgement and delicacy of feeling as those of janitresses and kept women... she has good reasons to wish to abolish Hell.

Charles Baudelaire (1821-67) on George Sand (1804-76)

What a hideous, odd-looking man Sydney Smith is! With a mouth like an oyster, and three double chins.

Mrs Brookfield on the Revd Sydney Smith (1771-1845)

Smug Sydney.

Lord Byron (1788-1824) on the Revd Sydney Smith

'on philosophers, analysts, God and the devil'

I must believe in the Apostolic Succession, there being no other way of accounting for the descent of the Bishop of Exeter from Judas Iscariot.

Revd Sydney Smith (1771-1845) on the Bishop of Exeter

❛on philosophers...❜

The truth is that Sydney Smith is naturally coarse, and a lover of scurrilous language.

John Ward, Earl of Dudley (1781-1833) on Revd Sydney Smith

My prayer to God is a very short one: 'Oh, Lord, make my enemies ridiculous.' God has granted it.

Voltaire (1694-1778)

God is the only being who, in order to rule, does not need even to exist.

Charles Baudelaire (1821-67)

You get the impression this is another dirty wop, an organ grinder.

W. H. Auden (1907-73) on Pope Pius XII (1875-1958)

Hume's philosophy, whether true or false, represents the bankruptcy of eighteenth-century reasonableness.

Bertrand Russell (1872-1970) on David Hume (1711-76), Scottish philosopher

The next time anyone asks you 'What is Bertrand Russell's Philosophy?' the correct answer is 'What year please?'

Sydney Hook on Bertrand Russell

Luther was the foulest of monsters.

Pope Gregory XV on Martin Luther (1483-1546)

The Lord strike him with madness and blindness. May the heavens empty upon him thunderbolts and the wrath of the Omnipotent burn itself unto him in the present and future world. May the Universe light against him and the earth open to swallow him up.

Pope Clement VI (1478-1534) on a now anonymous subject

... he stood on the flat road to heaven and buttered slides to hell for all the rest.

Oliver Wendell Holmes (1841-1935) on George Santayana (1863-1952), American philosopher

Voltaire, or the anti-poet – the king of nincompoops, the prince of the superficial, the anti-artist, the spokesman of janitresses.

Charles Baudelaire (1821-67) on Voltaire (1694-1778)

A liar and a father of lies.

Dante (1265-1321) on the Devil

⌜on philosophers...⌟

A philosophizing serpent.

Horace Walpole (1717-97), letterist and memoirist, on Mary
Wollstonecraft (1759-97), British feminist

She is an infidel... a vulgar and foolish one.

John Ruskin (1819-1900), art critic and author, on Harriet
Martineau (1802-76), British feminist and writer

Against Locke's philosophy I
think it an unanswerable
objection that, although he
carried his throat about with
him in this world for
seventy-two years, no man
ever condescended to cut it.

Thomas de Quincey (1785-1859), British
writer, in 'On Murder Considered As One
of the Fine Arts' (1827), on John Locke (1632-1704),
English philosopher

Actually I always loathed the Viennese
quack. I used to stalk him down dark alleys
of thought, and now we shall never forget
the sight of old, flustered Freud seeking to
unlock his door with the point of his
umbrella.

Vladimir Nabokov (1899-1977) on Sigmund Freud (1856-1939)

The bear loves licks and forms her young,
but bears are not philosophers.

Edmund Burke (1729-97) on Jean-Jacques Rousseau (1712-78)

... one of the most depraved, vicious and revolting humbugs who ever escaped from a nightmare or a lunatic asylum.

Preston Sturges on Aleister Crowley (1875-1947)

The arch-philistine Jeremy Bentham was the insipid, pedantic, leather-tongued oracle of the bourgeois intelligence of the nineteenth century.

Karl Marx (1818-83) on Jeremy Bentham (1748-1832), British political philospher

Maybe it would have been better if neither of us had been born.

Napoleon Bonaparte (1769-1821) on Jean-Jacques Rousseau (1712-78)

The Puritan hated bear-baiting, not because it gave pain to the bear, but because it gave pleasure to the spectators.

Thomas Babington Macaulay (1800-59), *History of England*

Plato is a bore.

Friedrich Wilhelm Nietzsche (1844-1900)

❲on philosophers...❳

If God were suddenly condemned to live the life which he has inflicted on men, he would kill himself.

Alexandre Dumas fils (1824-95)

Man is quite insane. He wouldn't know how to create a maggot, and he creates Gods by the dozen.

Michel de Montaigne (1533-92) on man

No one ever made more trouble than 'Gentle Jesus, meek and mild'.

James M. Gillis on Jesus

A parish Demagogue.

Percy Bysshe Shelley (1792-1822) on Jesus

Susan is lean, cadaverous and intellectual, with the proportions of a file and the voice of a hurdy-gurdy.

Anonymous writer in the *New York World* (1866) on Susan Bronwell Anthony (1820-1906), American feminist

I have no patience whatever with these Gorilla damnifications of humanity.

Thomas Carlyle (1795-1881) on Charles Darwin (1809-82)

A crazy fanatic... a crazy cranky being...
not only consistently dirty, but deplorably
dull ... A gloomy sort of ghoul ... blinking
like a stupid old owl.

Newspaper review of *Hedda Gabler* by Henrik Ibsen (1828-1906)

An ego like a raging tooth.

W. B. Yeats (1865-1939) on Mrs Patrick Campbell (1865-1940), actress

❛on the stage❜

Superabundance of foulness... wholly
immoral and degenerate... you cannot have
a clean pig stye.

Newspaper review of George Bernard Shaw's *Mrs Warren's Profession*

⎩on the stage⎭

Two things should be cut – the second act and the child's throat.

Noël Coward (1899-1973) on a dull play with an annoying child star

... his figure is that of a hippopotamus, his face like the bull and mouth on the panels of a heavy coach, his arms are fins flattened out of shape, his voice the gargling of an alderman with the quinsy and his acting altogether ought to be a natural, for it is certainly like nothing that Art has ever exhibited on stage.

Lord Byron (1788-1824) on Master William Betty (1791-1874), child actor

A woman whose face looked as if it had been made of sugar and someone had licked it.

George Bernard Shaw (1856-1950) on Isadora Duncan (1878-1927), American dancer

To me Edith looks like something that would eat its young.

Dorothy Parker (1893-1967) on Dame Edith Evans (1888-1976), British actress

My Dear Sir,
I have read your play.
Oh, my dear Sir.
Yours Faithfully

Henry Beerbohm Tree (1853-1917) to a would-be dramatist

Smells to high heaven. It is a dramatised stench.

Newspaper review of George Bernard Shaw's *Mrs Warren's Profession*

Foote is quite impartial, for he tells lies of everybody.

Samuel Johnson (1709-84) on Samuel Foote (1720-77), British actor and dramatist

... the ideal of the haberdashery clerk and of all the other chumps who had never heard of Rubens or the Greeks or fresh air.

Ralph Barton on Lillian Gish

He will ultimately take his stand in the
social rank... among the swindlers,
blacklegs, pickpockets and thimble-riggers
of his day.

Anonymous writer in *Tait's Edinburgh Magazine* (1855) on Phineas
Taylor Barnum (1810-91), American showman

She was so dramatic she stabbed the potatoes
at dinner.

Revd Sydney Smith (1771-1845) on Mrs Siddons (1755-1831),
tragedian actress

It was very good of God to let Carlyle and Mrs Carlyle marry one another and so make only two people miserable instead if four.

Samuel Butler (1835-1902) on Thomas Carlyle (1795-1881)

The majority of husbands remind me of an orang-utan trying to play the violin.

Honoré de Balzac (1799-1850)

❛on marriage❜

Marriage – a friendship recognised by the police.

Robert Louis Stevenson (1850-94) on marriage

❛on marriage❜

The music at a wedding procession always reminds me of the music of soldiers going into battle.

Heinrich Heine (1797-1856)

Unfaithful bitch! Messalina! Medusa! Gorgon!

Roman Emperor Claudius (10 BC-AD 54) on Valeria Messalina, his wife

She was a prymerole, a piggensye,
For any Lord to leggen in his bedde.
Or yet for any good yeman to wedde.

Geoffrey Chaucer (c.1343-1400), English poet

I bequeath all my property to my wife on the condition that she remarry immediately. Then there will be at least one man to regret my death.

Heinrich Heine (1797-1856) on his wife

Here lies my wife.
Here let her lie!
Now she's at rest, And so am I.

John Dryden (1631-1700), English poet, (proposed) 'Epitaph for his Wife'

Marriage is a desperate thing. The frogs in
Aesop were extreme wise; they had a great
mind to some water, but they would not
leap into the well, because they could not
get out again.

John Selden, English historian, in *Table Talk* (1689)

If you're afraid of loneliness, don't marry.

Anton Chekhov (1860-1904)

⸢on marriage⸥

It is embarrassing how he harps on his wife's dimensions: brave little heart, noble little creature, indomitable little soul – he only just stops short of 'wee cowering crimson-tippit Beastie.'

Sylvia Townsend Warner (1893-1978) on Thomas Carlyle (1795-1881)

You might people a colony with her; or give an assembly with her; or perhaps take your morning walks around her, always providing there were frequent resting places and you are in rude health. I was once rash enough to try walking around her before breakfast, but only got half way and gave up exhausted. Or you might read the Riot Act and disperse her; in short, you might do anything with her but marry her.

Revd Sydney Smith (1771-1845) on the news that an acquaintance was to marry a very overweight woman.

I could do without your face, Chloe, and without your neck, and your hands, and your limbs, and to save myself the trouble of mentioning the points in detail, I could do without you altogether.

Martial (c.40-104 AD), Roman poet

'on men, women and love'

Love is the affection of a mind that has nothing better to engage it.

Theophrastus, Greek philosopher (c. 372-287 BC)

⸢on men, women and love⸥

A word to you of Lady Caroline Lamb.
I speak from experience – keep clear of her
(I do not mean as a woman that is all fair).
She is a villainous intriguante in every
sense of the word, mad and malignant,
capable of all and every mischief. Above all,
guard your connections from her society.
With all her apparent absurdity, there is an
indefatigable and active spirit of meanness
and destruction about her which delights
and often succeeds in inflicting misery.

Lord Byron (1788-1824) writing to James Wedderburn Webster
about Lady Caroline Lamb

Love may arise from a generous sentiment –
namely, the liking for prostitution; but it
soons becomes corrupted by the liking for
ownership.

Charles Baudelaire (1821-67)

Woman is the opposite of the Dandy. That is
why she should be regarded with disgust...
woman is 'natural' – that is to say,
abominable. Moreover she is always vulgar –
that is to say the opposite of the Dandy.

Charles Baudelaire

There is only one way to be happy by means
of the heart – to have none.

Paul Bourget, French psychologist, in 1890

I have always been amazed that women are allowed to enter churches. What sort of conversations can they have with God?

Charles Baudelaire

Lord, she is Thin.

Anonymous, Annapolis County grave epitaph

Love, in present day society, is just the exchange of two momentary desires and the contact of two skins.

Nicholas Chamfort, French aphorist, in 1805

⟨on men, women and love⟩

Man remains what he has always been; the cruellest of all the animals, and the most elaborately and fiendishly sensual.

George Bernard Shaw (1856-1950) on men

She was never really charming until she died.

Terence (c.185-159 BC), epitaph to an unknown woman

Oh love will make a dog howl in tune.

Francis Beaumont and John Fletcher, playwrights, in 1608

Brigands demand your money or your life. Women demand both.

attr. Samuel Butler (1612-80)

... for although women might make excellent book-keepers, there is much in accountancy proper that is, we think, unsuitable for them.

English Institute of Chartered Accountants in *The Accountant* (1912)

【on men, women and love】

The more I see of men, the more I admire dogs.

Marie de Rabutin-Chantal, Marquise de Sévigné (1626-96)

A woman is only a woman,
But a good cigar is a smoke.

Rudyard Kipling (1865-1936), later used by Groucho Marx
(1895-1977)

The five worst infirmities that afflict the
female are indocility, discontent, slander,
jealousy and silliness.

Confucian marriage manual

The queen is most anxious to enlist every one who can speak or write to join in checking this mad wicked folly of 'Woman's Rights' with all its attendant horrors, on which her poor feeble sex is bent, forgetting every sense of womanly feeling and propriety.

Queen Victoria
(1819-1901)

# 	on men, women and love

There is but one thing in the world worse than a shameless woman and that's another woman.

Aristophanes (c.448-c.380 BC) in *Thesmophoriazusae*

Such is the human race. Often it does seem a pity that Noah and his party didn't miss the boat.

Mark Twain (1835-1910)

A man is in general better pleased when he has a good dinner upon his table, than when his wife talks Greek.

Samuel Johnson (1709-1840)

If you pick up a starving dog and make him prosperous, he will not bite you. That is the principal difference between a dog and a man.

Mark Twain (1835-1910)

The male is by nature superior, and the female inferior: the one rules and the other is ruled.

Aristotle (384-322 BC), in *Politics*

Too often the strong silent man is silent because he does not know what to say, and is reputed strong only because he has remained silent.

Winston Churchill (1874-1965)

Man originates in muck, wades a while in muck, makes muck and in the end returns to muck.

Johann Christoff Friedrich von Schiller (1759-1805), German playwright, in *The Robbers* (1781)

I sometimes think that God, in creating man, somewhat overestimated his ability.

Oscar Wilde (1854-1900)

It is only the man whose intellect is clouded by his sexual impulses that could give the name of 'the fair sex' to that undersized, narrow-shouldered, broad-hipped and short-legged race.

Artur Schopenhauer (1788-1860), German philosopher

Once a woman has given you her heart you can never get rid of the rest of her body.

John Vanbrugh (1664-1726), British playwright, in *The Relapse* (1696)

❴on men, women and love❵

The history of women is the history of the worst tyranny the world has ever known: the tyranny of the weak over the strong. It is the only tyranny that ever lasts.

Oscar Wilde (1854-1900)

Their slanderous tongues are so short, and the time wherein they have lavished out their words freely hath been so long, that they know we cannot catch hold of them to pull them out, and they think we will not write to reprove their lying lips.

Jane Anger in *Protection for Women* (1589)

A 'Grand Old Man.' That means on our continent anyone with snow-white hair who has kept out of jail until eighty.

Stephen Leacock, English-born Canadian humorist, in 1910

God created Adam, lord of all living creatures, but Eve spoiled it all.

Martin Luther (1483-1546)

I consider that women who are authors,
lawyers and politicians are monsters.

Auguste Renoir (1840-1919)

The dissoluteness of our lascivious, impudent,
rattle-pated gadding females is now such...
they are lowde and stubborne; their feet
abide not in their houses; now they are
without, now in the streets, and lie in wait
in every corner; being never well pleased
nor contented, but when they are wandering
abroad to Playes, the Playhouses, Dancing-
Matches, Masques and publick Shewes.

William Prynne (1600-69), English pamphleteer

❬on men, women and love❭

Twenty million young women rose to their feet with the cry 'We will not be dictated to' and promptly became stenographers.

G. K. Chesterton (1874-1936)

Mrs Balinger is one of those ladies who pursue Culture in bands, as though it were dangerous to meet it alone.

Edith Wharton (1862-1937), American novelist

How unpleasant to meet Mr Eliot!
With his features of clerical cut,
And his brow so grim
And his mouth so prim
And his conversation, so nicely
Restricted to What Precisely
And If and Perhaps and But.

T. S. Eliot (1888-1965) on himself in Five Finger Exercises

⸢on oneself⸥

When I don't look like the tragic muse, I look like the smoky relic of the great Boston Fire.

Louisa May Alcott (1832-88) on herself

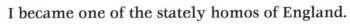

He was meddling too much in my private life.

Tennessee Williams (1911-83) on why he had stopped visiting his psychoanalyst

I became one of the stately homos of England.

Quentin Crisp, writer and actor, on himself

'on oneself'

You have but two topics, yourself and me and I'm sick of both.

Samuel Johnson (1709-84) on James Boswell (1740-95),
British author and biographer

I think I may boast myself to be, with all possible vanity, the most unlearned and uninformed female who ever dared to be an authoress.

Jane Austen (1775-1817)
on herself, to the Revd
James Clarke

Somebody's boring me. I think it's me.

Dylan Thomas (1914-53)

If people only knew as much about painting as I do, they would never buy my pictures.

Sir Edwin Henry Landseer (1802-73) to W. P. Frith

My handwriting looks as if a swarm of ants, escaping from an ink bottle, had walked over a sheet of paper without wiping their legs.

Revd Sydney Smith (1771-1845)

Page numbers printed in bold indicate insulting references to or on the subject, other page numbers indicate insulting remarks made by the subject.

`index`

❮index❯